PRAIRIE ODDITIES

Punkinhead, Peculiar Gravity, and More Lesser Known Histories

DARREN
BERNHARDT

GREAT PLAINS PRESS

Great Plains Publications
320 Rosedale Ave
Winnipeg, MB R3L 1L8
www.greatplainspress.ca

Great Plains Publications gratefully acknowledges the financial support provided
for its publishing program by the Government of Canada through the Canada
Book Fund; the Canada Council for the Arts; the Province of Manitoba through
the Book Publishing Tax Credit and the Book Publisher Marketing Assistance
Program; and the Manitoba Arts Council.

Design & Typography by Relish Ideas Inc.
Printed in Canada by Friesens

Library and Archives Canada Cataloguing in Publication

Title: Prairie oddities: punkinhead, peculiar gravity and more lesser known
    histories / Darren Bernhardt.
Names: Bernhardt, Darren, 1970- author.
Identifiers: Canadiana (print) 20240388313 | Canadiana (ebook) 2024038833X |
    ISBN 9781773371221 (softcover) | ISBN 9781773371238 (EPUB)
Subjects: LCSH: Prairie Provinces—History—Anecdotes.
Classification: LCC FC3237 .B47 2024 | DDC 971.2—dc23

Canadä

To my family—Jennifer, Abigail and Benjamin—
who encompass my past, present and future.
And who are always enthralled by my stories.
Right? Right?

Looking south along Memorial Boulevard in 1947. The photographer would have been standing between Hudson's Bay (left) and where the Winnipeg Art Gallery is today (right).

PROVINCIAL ARCHIVES OF MANITOBA N18056

BELLS OF ST. BONIFACE

On a sweltering July afternoon in 1968, a carelessly flicked-away cigarette landed in dry-as-dust wood-chip insulation where it smouldered briefly, began to glow, and then erupted.

It took just moments for the ravenous flames to roar into an inferno that consumed St. Boniface Cathedral and silenced the bells that first rang nearly a hundred and thirty years prior, when most of the Northwest was still unblemished by European settlement.

That midday blaze rendered the bells into a molten mass inside the ruins of the cathedral on the Red River's east bank, near downtown Winnipeg. It put an exclamation point on a storied history of the trio of bells, which had averted disaster once before. They had been toppled—and partially melted—in an 1860 fire as well. And before they ever arrived in St. Boniface, in 1840, they criss-crossed the Atlantic Ocean multiple times and were responsible for what is believed to be the first-ever workers' strike in the Northwest.

22 JUILLET, 1968

St. Boniface Cathedral engulfed in flames
in July 1968 CATHEDRALESTBONIFACE.CA

ABOVE The original 1819 bell commissioned by Lord Selkirk as it appears on display in Le Musée de Saint-Boniface Museum DARREN BERNHARDT

Joseph-Norbert Provencher
SOCIETE HISTORIQUE DE SAINT-BONIFACE ARCHIVES/COLLECTION GENERALE DE SHSB, SHSB 497

THE FIRST BELL

Father Joseph-Norbert Provencher established a Roman Catholic mission on the riverbank site shortly after arriving in the Red River Colony at Fort Douglas (near the present-day Alexander Docks in Winnipeg) from Quebec in July 1818. Provencher's little poplar-log building, 50 feet by 30 feet, stood on what is now the middle of Taché Avenue but was then a small dirt road. It was just steps from where the grand cathedral would later be built—and across the river from what would become the birthplace of Winnipeg at the confluence of the Red and Assiniboine rivers.

The land for the mission was donated by the fort's namesake, Thomas Douglas, better known as Lord Selkirk. Selkirk, who established the colony in 1811 but only visited it one time, in 1817, initially granted twenty acres for Provencher's mission site. He later granted another 15,000 acres for a settlement that eventually became the city of St. Boniface (which amalgamated with Winnipeg in the 1970s).

In addition to the land, Selkirk also granted sound. He was in poor health in 1818 when he made plans to leave England and spend that winter in France. Before doing so, he ordered a single bell from the Whitechapel Bell Foundry in London, England, and arranged for its blessing by a bishop before it was shipped to Red River. In 1856, Whitechapel would cast Big Ben and the four smaller bells that still ring inside the tower of the great clock at the Palace of Westminster.

"...the first bell that tolled in Red River since creation"

Margaret Arnett MacLeod,
***Bells of the Red River*, 1937**

The hundred-pound chime commissioned by Selkirk was stamped with 1819, the year it was molded and transported across the ocean to become "the first bell that tolled in Red River since creation," Margaret Arnett MacLeod wrote in her 1937 book, *Bells of the Red River.*

It was a simple bell but served a great purpose. Food had been scarce in the settlement and the cool autumn winds had arrived. The bell's clangor, heard at the Hudson's Bay Company and North-West Company forts across the river, rang in a new day and renewed hope, MacLeod wrote.

Peter Rindisbacher's painting, *Winter Fishing on the Ice of the Assynoibain and Red River*, 1821. The second St. Boniface church and its bell tower can be seen just to the right of the tree in the centre of the image. Fort Gibraltar stands on the hill just to the left of the trees at the confluence of the Red and Assiniboine rivers. HISTORICAL ATLAS OF CANADA

It also signalled the importance of Provencher's small mission, which served as residence, school, and chapel. In November, the site and surrounding land was consecrated by Provencher as Saint Boniface.

The name honoured an eighth-century Benedictine monk, who was born in 675 with a given name that varies in historical reports as Winfred, Winfrid, Wynfrid and Wynfrith. He spent thirty-five years spreading the Catholic faith through Germany during the Dark Ages, preaching, teaching, and building schools, monasteries, and convents. His name was changed in 716 by Pope Gregory II to Boniface, which means "a man who does good deeds."

Catholic legend credits Boniface as the founder of the Christmas tree tradition, although that first one was an oak tree. It had been dedicated by pagans to the Norse god of thunder, Thor, and legend had it that no one could cut it down. So along came Boniface, who felled it to show Christianity's strength in an attempt to convert the pagans.

In full service to its namesake, Provencher's St. Boniface chapel became a focal point for missionary work in the Northwest. As the first permanent mission west of the Great Lakes, it also served as the cornerstone of francophone settlement in the region.

The second St. Boniface church, started in 1819 and completed a few years later, was made of oak and measured 80 feet by 35 feet. This is an 1823 sketch by William Kemp. PROVINCIAL ARCHIVES OF MANITOBA, N10736

The mission, which grew into its own diocese and later, archdiocese, covered a vast region in its early days. Its territory stretched from northwestern Ontario south to the US state of Kentucky and west through Manitoba to the Pacific coast. Provencher's St. Boniface became known as the Mother Church in Western Canada.

The original building was soon replaced by a larger church, 33 feet by 100 feet, construction for which began in 1819 but wasn't completed until 1825. That church became a cathedral in 1822 when the Archdiocese of Quebec declared Provencher an auxiliary bishop. The auxiliary was an envoy to the Archbishop of Quebec City, who couldn't administer Red River or lands farther west on his own.

The archbishop hurried the process to create a diocese in the area before the Anglicans. John West had arrived in Red River in 1820 and built the West's first Anglican church in 1822, the forerunner to St. John's Cathedral.

In light of the rapidly expanding distinction of the St. Boniface mission, Provencher immediately

Leading the Way: Firsts in the Northwest 1807-1859

1807
January 6: Birth of Lereine (Reine) Lagimodière, believed to be the first European child born in the Northwest.

It happens at Fort Pembina, a trading post of the North West Company (NWCo). Today it is Pembina, North Dakota. Back then it was part of Rupert's Land, a vast area claimed by the Hudson's Bay Company as part of its fur trading monopoly (a monopoly that the North West Company, and other freelance traders, just ignored). Pembina was

Jean-Baptiste Lagimodière
SOCIÉTÉ HISTORIQUE DE SAINT-BONIFACE

ceded to the US as part of the Treaty of 1818, when the international border was established.

Model of Provencher's cathedral in Le Musée de Saint-Boniface Museum DARREN BERNHARDT

set about planning a new, purpose-built cathedral. He travelled to Lower Canada (Quebec) in 1830 to raise enough money to start the project. He was gone for a year and a half, and when he returned to St. Boniface in June 1832, he had to wait another year for masons from Lower Canada to arrive. The only ones in Red River were employed by the Hudson's Bay Company and unavailable.

The work began in 1833 but continued to run into delays due to a lack of materials or money to keep going—often both at the same time. To help the construction along, Provencher carried stone and hoisted it up the scaffolding himself.

The monumental stone edifice was girded by two turrets that could be seen for far distances from either side of the Red River. For his efforts, the church became known by the people in Red River as Provencher's Cathedral. However, the most anticipated piece was yet to arrive.

Additional funds raised by Provencher, combined with monetary gifts from friends in Quebec, covered the 101 British pounds—about $175 Canadian—for a trio of bells that weighed more than 1,600 pounds. Provencher arranged for couriers to receive the bells at York Factory on Hudson Bay and transport them inland, down the Red River to St. Boniface—a 1,127-kilometre trek.

The men fought against the current, straining with the enormous weight of the bells. At other times they dragged the loaded boats with thick rope or lifted everything—boats and cargo—across shallow rapids or a myriad of portages. By the time they approached Norway House, just north of Lake Winnipeg, they had crossed thirty-four portages and the burden proved too much. They had enough. They went on strike—the first known workers' strike in the West—and refused to carry the bells any further.

Provencher turned to Andrew McDermot, a merchant who owned a brigade of boats, to retrieve everything. The bells arrived and were unloaded from their crates in time for All Saints' Day, November 1, 1840, when they sounded for

Reine is born to Jean-Baptiste Lagimodière and Marie-Anne Gaboury, who are part of a Métis buffalo hunting community in the area, and who would play key roles in Manitoba's history.

In 1811, the family—now consisting of Lagimodière and Gaboury and four children—moves north to help establish what becomes Lord Selkirk's Red River Colony, an agricultural settlement he names Assiniboia, on land granted from the HBC. Selkirk had bought enough HBC shares to become part owner and his first group of settlers set up around what is now Kildonan

Reine Lagimodière
SOCIÉTÉ HISTORIQUE DE SAINT-BONIFACE

Park. The name Kildonan is in honour of the parish in Sutherlandshire, Scotland, from which many settlers came.

By setting his colony along key fur trade routes, Selkirk attempts to cut off the HBC's rival NWCo. His

Painting by Ernest J. Hutchins, called Old Fort Douglas, Red River 1815 LIBRARY AND ARCHIVES CANADA

efforts enrage the NWCo., which terrorizes his colonists and persuades many to leave. As the turbulence increases and the colony is threatened, Lagimodière heads to Montreal in October 1815 to alert Selkirk.

Tensions culminate in the June 19, 1816, Battle of Seven Oaks, which leaves HBC Governor Robert Semple and twenty of his men dead. Led by Cuthbert Grant, the NWCo. take possession of Fort Douglas. Gaboury is given refuge by Chief Peguis, who goes out the next morning to gather the dead from the battlefield and bury them

the first time—though they were not yet installed in the cathedral's tower.

THE BELLS RING ACROSS THE PRAIRIE

In 1843, a decade after the start of construction, Provencher wrote that his church still had "no vault, no spire, and the plastering still to be done," according to MacLeod. In 1846, an update from Provencher noted one spire was finished and the other was being built.

"Those early settlers had only crude colour and sound to break the bleakness of their endless wilds, and musical sound, even the rhythmic scraping of a homemade fiddle, was dearly prized," MacLeod wrote in her book. "So, one can imagine the joy that the musical bells sounding the notes of F, G, and A, brought to beauty-starved Red River."

There is no record of when the bells were finally installed, but it is known they were in place by 1849, when they rang for mass on Ascension Day. On that day, hundreds of armed Métis, led by Louis Riel Sr., were on their way to demand the

"One can imagine the joy that the musical bells sounding the notes of F, G, and A, brought to beauty-starved Red River."

Margaret Arnett MacLeod, *Bells of the Red River*, 1937

release from jail of Pierre-Guillaume (William) Sayer, who was charged with violating the Hudson's Bay Company's charter by illegally trafficking in furs. When the bells sounded, the men immediately headed to the church, stacked their guns outside, and went to mass.

In 1857, a twelve-year-old Louis Riel Jr. received his first communion at the cathedral, which also became the site of his funeral and his final resting place after his hanging in 1885. The bells rang for him both times.

Provencher's beloved bells also tolled when he died in 1853.

under trees along the banks of Logan's Creek, just north of the present-day Alexander Docks. Lagimodière, meanwhile, is taken prisoner by Nor'Westers on his return to the colony and imprisoned in Fort William (now Thunder Bay). He's not reunited with Gaboury until September 1816.

Selkirk makes his first and only trip to Red River in June 1817, bringing a regiment. The soldiers recapture the fort and Selkirk sets about rebuilding the colony. For their efforts, Lagimodière and Gaboury are granted land by Selkirk on the east bank of the Red River, where

they build a house and continue to expand their family. Among their children is Julie Lagimodière, the future mother of Louis Riel.

Gaboury is often referred to as the Mother of Red River for her help in establishing the colony and because many Métis people of the Prairies can trace their ancestry to her. Lagimodière Boulevard in Winnipeg is named in honour of Jean-Baptiste.

Peguis, in 1817, was one of five Saulteaux and Cree chiefs to sign a treaty with Selkirk, the first agreement permitting farmland access to settlers in western Canada. The HBC and

NWCo. merge in 1821 under the HBC banner.

1820
September 9: First baptism on record.

The child is William, son of Thomas and Phoebe Bunn. Thomas is an accountant at Rock Depot, an HBC depot on the Hayes River, about 90 kilometres west of present-day Shamattawa. The Bunns' marriage, earlier that same year, is the first Protestant wedding in what was to become western Canada. It, and the baptism, are performed by Rev. John West.

1822
October: The first Anglican church opens for worship.

Constructed by Rev. John West, it is a small wooden chapel about two kilometres north of Fort Douglas.

The little mission is built along the western bank of a curve in the Red River, near where a small stream flows under the spread of heavy elm trees and twisted willows. Immediately south of the chapel is a cemetery established in 1812 by the first group of Selkirk settlers.

The chapel would come to be known as The Upper Church and later

THE FIRST CATHEDRAL FIRE

In 1860, the cathedral burned to the ground. The bells crashed into the ruins. According to the *Nor'Wester* newspaper, the fire started on December 14, 1860, when two girls were making candles for an upcoming funeral mass. They were in the kitchen of Bishop Alexandre-Antonin Taché's house, which was attached to the cathedral. Taché had taken over the diocese after Provencher's death.

The girls were cooking bison tallow in a large kettle on a stove to render the fat for the candles. It boiled over and immediately began to burn when it contacted the hot stove. The panicked girls tried to move the kettle but spilled more, fuelling the flames. They then threw water onto the grease fire, but that exacerbated the problem.

Boards that were to be used to build the coffin for the upcoming funeral had been set near the stove to dry. They caught fire and soon the house was engulfed. Before long, the flames leapt to the cathedral.

"The scene presented a wild grandeur—flames rolling hither and thither—sweeping upwards 50 or 100 feet and enveloping the edifice," The *Nor'Wester* reported on December 17, 1860. "Fanned by a strong south wind, the fire burned around the steeples fiercely. At length, the great belfry began to totter, and away went one steeple, to be soon after followed by the other."

Taché, who was away on missionary work, returned in late February 1861 and "knelt in the midst of the ruins," the paper reported. In doing so,

The third St. Boniface church, built between 1832-1839 and destroyed by a fire in 1860, is seen in 1858 from what would be the current-day riverwalk at The Forks. It shows the grandeur and influence it exerted over the young settlement. HUMPHREY LLOYD HIME/PROVINCIAL ARCHIVES OF MANITOBA

he found the bells, battered somewhat and slightly melted, but not beyond repair. About a thousand pounds of metal was salvaged. It was packed and sent back to Whitechapel, via Hudson Bay and the Atlantic Ocean, to be recast.

Taché then set off on a "begging tour of Lower Canada" giving emotionally heavy sermons that brought tears and donations from those attending. Once again, stonemasons and carpenters from Quebec came out to begin construction on yet

as St. John's Cathedral. It falls victim to the great flood of 1826, when it is heaved from its foundation and washed away. The flood also destroys the original cemetery.

The present church, built in 1926 in the Luxton neighbourhood of Winnipeg on Anderson Avenue near Main Street, is the fourth one on the site. The location of the original chapel, considered the birthplace of the Anglican Church in Western Canada, is near the southeast corner of the present cemetery. The brook that ran nearby has long since been filled in, save for a bit of gully at the riverbank. The oldest marked grave in the cemetery dates to 1832 and is that of eight-month-old George Simpson, son of George and Francis Ramsay Simpson, the Governor of the Hudson's Bay Company and his wife.

1833

First piano in the Northwest is brought from London by Mary Lowman, a newly arrived teacher at the Red River Academy, a school established In 1832 near St. John's Cathedral.

Lowman married retired Hudson Bay Company chief factor James Curtis Bird, whose estate north of

Mary Lowman
ARCHIVES OF MANITOBA

present-day Winnipeg is still known as Birds Hill.

The school was later to be renamed St. John's College and would eventually merge with Ravenscourt School to create St. John's-Ravenscourt School, now located in Winnipeg's Wildwood Park neighbourhood.

1845

September 6: The first-known execution in the Red River Settlement occurs.

Capinesseweet, a Saulteaux, is hanged for the murder of Patungao'kaysnay, a Sioux. Capinesseweet allegedly shot Patungao'kaysnay at Fort Garry on July 31 as revenge for the death of his father, who had been killed by a Sioux warrior a year earlier.

Capinesseweet was convicted by a jury in the General Quarterly Court of Assiniboine, the sentence of death ordered by Adam Thom, "the first recorder of Rupert's Land."

another cathedral, the corner-stone for which was blessed by Taché in April 1863. The new design, smaller than its pre-decessor due to a tighter budget (the church was still in debt from Provencher's cathedral), eschewed twin spires in favour of a single tower.

The fourth St. Boniface church, circa 1890 PROVINCIAL ARCHIVES OF MANITOBA, N3451

Cathédrale (troisième) - 1863.

CRISS-CROSSING THE ATLANTIC

The bells, meanwhile, were in the midst of another adventure. The ship carrying them back to North America hit a storm off Newfoundland. Instead of making its way to the Hudson Strait and into the bay, the ship took refuge at St. John's. The bells were unloaded and sent to Portland, Maine, then by rail and boat to Duluth, Minnesota.

Taché found it cost-prohibitive and too oner-ous to use oxcart to move the bells the remaining 700 kilometres to St. Boniface. So they were sent back to the east coast and onto the next ship back to London.

Thom is not a judge but an employee of HBC, which is responsible for the administration of justice in Rupert's Land.

Roy St. George Stubbs, in his book the *Four Recorders of Rupert's Land*, noted Thom lacked jurisdiction to pass that sentence and "it may well be that the first execution in Red River was a wanton miscarriage of justice."

1850

December 22: Henry Budd is ordained a deacon, becoming the first Indigenous person in North America to be admitted to the ministry of the Church of England.

Henry Budd PROVINCIAL ARCHIVES OF MANITOBA

Born in 1812 in Norway House, his name is Sakachuwescam, which in Cree means "Going up the hill." His father Muskego Budd is Swampy Cree, and his Métis mother is Washesoow'sque (also called Agathus or Mary) Cocking.

Muskego dies before Budd is born. At age 10, Budd is put into the care of

On the other side of the Atlantic, they were transferred to another ship and returned via the northern route into Hudson Bay. They arrived at York Factory in 1863 but remained there for a year before making their way to St. Boniface.

It's not clear why they sat there that long. It's possible no one was eager to take up the challenge of transporting them again. The diocese's early archives, which might have documented the reason, were lost in the 1860 fire.

After the bells arrived, Taché insisted the debt on them be cleared before they could ring again. Residents in Red River—Catholic and Protestant alike—were so eager to have them back that together they raised the outstanding funds. Though the bells weren't yet set in the spire, that part of the church being still under construction, the bells chimed again on Christmas Eve 1864 from their temporary home in the wooden scaffolding at the south side of the church.

The bells were blessed in March 1865 and given names. Many names, in fact, after some of the children in the settlement. Norbert Joseph Florent

The bells were blessed in March 1865 and given names. Many names, in fact, after some of the children in the settlement.

Henriette Sophie was one bell. The other was Vital Frances Louise Jane Nancy, and the third was James Edwards Jeanne.

It was anticipated that the steeple to house the bells would be finished in summer 1868, but a violent July storm set that back. It ripped through the settlement, wrecking several structures including the steeple.

The encore to that disaster was years of famine, damage caused by floods and frosts, and even locusts, which put a dent in the church's finances. It wasn't until 1883, the year St. Boniface was incorporated as a town, that the bells made their way into the new steeple.

missionary Rev. John West, who baptizes him July 21, 1822, and renames him.

Budd attends missionary school and establishes missions in The Pas, Manitoba, and at Cumberland House and Fort-de-la-Corne in Saskatchewan. His translations of scriptural writings into Cree are used for many years in northern Manitoba and Saskatchewan.

He is ordained to the priesthood on June 10, 1853, three years after becoming a deacon.

1853
James Bruce introduces the first threshing machine

Red River Settlement house in what is now Kildonan Park, 1919 PROVINCIAL ARCHIVES OF MANITOBA/GEORGE HARRIS FONDS

in Canada. He brings it back on a ox-drawn cart from St. Paul, Minnesota to the Red River Settlement. For years, his services are in demand all over the West. Bruce, who was born in 1933 in what is now Kildonan Park, also introduces matches into Canada in place of the flint stone.

Drawing of the *Anson Northup* (no date) PROVINCIAL ARCHIVES OF MANITOBA

1859

June 10: The whistle of the first steamboat is heard in the Red River Settlement—followed by cannon fire.

The *Anson Northup* (commonly misspelled Northrup), named in honour of her owner and captain, departs from Fort Abercrombie, Dakota Territory (North Dakota), on June 6 and reaches the HBC post of Upper Fort Garry on June 10.

The commander of the British force at the fort orders the firing of the cannon in honour of the event. The British flag is hoisted to greet the Stars and Stripes flag on the *Northup*, and the bells of St. Boniface Cathedral ring out.

"One day at last, the celebrated bells of St. Boniface pealed forth from their belfry above the front door of the church, inviting by their sweet and far-reaching sounds the travellers on our prairies to prayer, meditation, and the memory of their departed ones," wrote Louis Arthur Prud'homme, a lawyer, judge, historian, author, and politician in Manitoba between 1881-1941. "I have called them celebrated and truly these dear bells are not at all commonplace."

MOST IMPOSING CHURCH IN WESTERN CANADA

By 1904, as the population of Catholics in western Canada boomed, plans were drawn up for the biggest cathedral yet. There were 12,000 Catholics in the region in 1881 and 20,000 by 1888. In St. Boniface, the numbers more than doubled from 2,154 in 1888 to 4,615 in 1906, where construction began on the new edifice.

"This new building is a necessity. Our children alone fill the current cathedral," said Bishop Louis Philippe Adélard Langevin, who blessed

The St. Boniface Cathedral—the fifth church on the site—is seen being built, circa 1908, behind the fourth one. PROVINCIAL ARCHIVES OF MANITOBA

The circular stained glass window of the St.Boniface Cathedral can be seen in this archival image. UNIVERSITY OF ST. BONIFACE ARCHIVES

the cornerstone on August 15, 1906. Langevin was the successor to Taché, who died in 1894, and he oversaw construction of what became the most imposing church in Western Canada.

As the highest Catholic authority in the growing west, the new cathedral needed to be far more extravagant than Taché's budget model. The design called for the return of the palatial twin spires that soared 150 feet to domed cupolas, with a twenty-five-foot diameter stained-glass rose window set between them above the main entrance, which featured three arched doorways. The rose window cast light into the sanctuary from a vaulted ceiling seventy feet high. The building, which could accommodate a congregation of 2,050, was 100 feet wide between the bases of the two towers, and 312 feet long. And it was all covered in limestone. Just as elaborate was the bill. It cost $325,000 (nearly $11 million today), which was borrowed over a forty-year term.

It opened in 1908 with the bells given a place of honour, lined up together in one of the towers. It was the same year St. Boniface became a city and, for a time, was referred to as the Cathedral City because of its landmark.

The cathedral even earned the title of minor basilica, an extremely rare designation. It was decreed in June 1949 by Pope Pius because its style echoed that of historical Roman basilicas. But its lack of transepts and cupola, considered essential basilica elements, prevented it from earning full status.

DISASTER FROM A CIGARETTE

The bells chimed for six decades until that day of the flicked cigarette, when the St. Boniface community gathered to mark the 150th anniversary of Provencher's first mission.

At noon on July 22, 1968, workers were sprucing up the cathedral, doing some reshingling, painting, and other minor work on the towers. As they broke for lunch, one of them made that fateful flick. They climbed down the ladders and

Smoke rises from the ruins of the cathedral on July 22, 1968. UNIVERSITY OF MANITOBA ARCHIVES/ *WINNIPEG TRIBUNE* COLLECTION

were on the ground for only a few minutes before flames were leaping from the roof. The twin turrets turned into burning torch heads.

The heat blew out the colossal stained-glass window while the flames fed on the spires until they weakened and toppled through the cathedral's roof. The collapsed spires tore at the belltowers and carried them down as well. When the flames were finally extinguished, all that remained were the exterior stone walls, including the facade and the sacristy (the room where a priest prepares for a service).

It was all gone in three hours. The heat was so intense it could be felt two blocks away, according to media reports. A piece of the roof was later found in the backyard of a house 500 metres from the cathedral, presumably propelled there by the force of the towers collapsing. The bells were completely melted.

Philippe Mailhot, former director of the St. Boniface Museum near the cathedral, witnessed the blaze. When the bells fell, Mailhot told Laval University historian David Girard "a great

The boat takes a daytrip with passengers to Lower Fort Garry, 30 kilometres north on the Red River, on June 13, then returns to Fort Abercrombie on June 17. The excursion proves steamboat navigation on the Red is feasible and ignites a new era.

An 1857 agreement with the US allows HBC to move goods through that country, making shipping easier for the company. But it spells the end for York Factory on the southwestern shore of Hudson Bay, which had been the HBC's headquarters and primary supply depot since 1684. York Factory could only receive vessels once a year. And being 900 kilometres northeast of Upper Fort Garry, everything was then hauled south on a difficult journey through rivers and portages.

With the emergence of the new US route, York Factory's role effectively ended in 1873 and the headquarters title was transferred to Upper Fort Garry.

July-August: The first hotel in the Northwest, The Royal, is opened by Henry McKenney, shortly after he arrives at Fort Garry aboard the steamship *Anson Northup* from Minnesota.

He buys an old log building from Andrew

McDermot, who owns several buildings scattered around an area east of what is now Main Street and north of present-day Lombard Avenue.

McDermot's land is among the largest allotments at nearly 260 metres wide—from today's McDermot Avenue to about the middle of Portage Avenue and stretching from the river into what is now the Exchange District. McDermot called his property Emerald Lodge, presumably in honour of his Republic of Ireland birthplace, while others referred to it as McDermotown.

McKenney turns the structure he bought—somewhere between Owen (now McDermot) and Post Office streets (now Lombard Avenue), and along a rough trail several hundred feet east of Main—into The Royal.

McKenney could foresee the influx of visitors, settlers and businesspeople that would come with the commencement of direct steamboat service. A couple of years later, he obtains the first liquor licence in the West and opens the first bar. He later adds a general store. By spring 1862, his businesses have prospered so much that McKenney makes a decision that changes the course of development in the area and sets the future for Winnipeg (see: June 2, 1862).

November 1: The first newspaper printing press in the Northwest arrives in Red River, and on December 28, 1859, the first issue of the *Nor'Wester* is published.

William Coldwell and William Buckingham set up their press in a small building a little south of the corner of Main Road and Schultz Street (later Water Avenue). The spot is now a parking lot on the street, renamed William Stephenson Way.

Coldwell had been a correspondent for the *Toronto Leader* while Buckingham was a parliamentary reporter for *The Globe* in the same city. Both came looking for fresh starts in a land they believed was poised for growth.

The *Nor'Wester* is the first to use the name Winnipeg on its masthead on February 24, 1866, seven years before the city was incorporated. Prior to that, the masthead identified the paper as representing the Red River Settlement.

The paper lasts until November 24, 1869, when Louis Riel suppressed it during the uprisings in the settlement.

cry went up from the crowd and we all felt that we were witnessing the end of something."

Parishioners stepped up with a willingness to take on debt and rebuild the cathedral exactly as it was, but when estimates exceeded $10 million, and with church attendance sliding, a decision was made to build a smaller structure. Franco-Manitoban architect Étienne Gaboury was awarded the $630,000 contract and his design, half the size of what once existed, was built within the remaining walls.

The hybrid cathedral opened in July 1972, the year St. Boniface was absorbed into the city of Winnipeg. It blends old and new, allowing visitors to walk through the arches of the old facade into a stone-and-steel courtyard before transitioning to the newer structure. It was designated a provincial heritage site in February 1994.

Though some elements of the old cathedral found their way into the new one, other parts of the structure found their way to the St. Boniface Museum. That building houses some pieces of marble from the cathedral's altar, the clappers

One of the spires of the St. Boniface Cathedral is seen as it collapses and falls away. SOCIÉTÉ HISTORIQUE DE SAINT-BONIFACE SHSB26303

that struck the bells to make them ring, old tools used on stonework in the construction, and a jar of charred wood. The bells are gone but their song lives on. A recording of their music had been made days before the fire at another outdoor service marking the 150th anniversary.

Coldwell later started up a couple of other short-lived newspapers, *Red River Pioneer* and *The Manitoban*. The latter merged with the *Manitoba Free Press*.

December 19: The first booksellers in the Northwest open shop. William Coldwell and William Buckingham of the *Nor'Wester* advertise that their "stock of books is varied and extensive."

December 20: Dr. Curtis Bird opens practice as the first medical practitioner in the West. His shop is at the corner of Main Street and Bannatyne Avenue in what will become Winnipeg.

Curtis Bird's house and drugstore, seen at lower left, at the southeast corner of Bannatyne Avenue and Main Street, in 1875
CITY OF WINNIPEG ARCHIVES

LOST BELL FOUND

As for that original single bell from Lord Selkirk, it fell into the shadow of history. In poor health and struggling financially, Selkirk was on his way back to England when he died in spring 1820 in France. The bell remained the only public gift he made to the colony he founded. And it was lost.

According to MacLeod, Provencher's first chapel had a tower, so presumably the bell was hung there. But there is no record of that. In fact, there was nothing written about the bell after its arrival in 1819.

That prompted MacLeod to go looking. Though nearly a hundred years of the bell's history had passed by the time MacLeod began her sleuthing, she had faith. She spent years ascending church towers in Manitoba and descending through trapdoors into musty cellars and storage areas. She tracked down bells sent from Manitoba to Quebec, and every time she thought she might be close, she was left disappointed.

Eventually, MacLeod set her efforts aside and focused on other things. A chance conversation in the mid-1930s, fifteen years after starting her search, revived the hope. An elderly woman overheard

MacLeod lamenting her failures. The woman told MacLeod about a cracked bell that used to be in the yard of the Roman Catholic Church in St. François Xavier, west of Winnipeg. The bell was a familiar sight in the tall grass just off the path the woman had walked as a young girl going to catechism.

MacLeod eagerly met with the priest, J.V. Fyfe, but he had not heard of the bell. Thumbing through church records dating to 1824, he found no mention of it. But after a few minutes of sitting and thinking, Fyfe recalled seeing what he thought was a bell in the basement. Fyfe sent someone down with a flashlight and ten minutes later, MacLeod's years of searching were over. The bell was covered with thick dust and dirt obscured the stamped date, but it was finally recovered.

The Parish of St. François Xavier is the second-oldest Roman Catholic parish between Lake Superior and the Pacific Ocean, having been established by Provencher 1823. It is assumed the bell was passed on to that church in 1840, when the trio of new bells arrived in St. Boniface. It rang in St. François Xavier for three decades but had not been listed in any records as Lord Selkirk's bell.

The 1868 storm that tore down the steeple of Taché's church in St. Boniface also ripped Selkirk's bell from its tower in St. Francois Xavier and threw it into the cemetery, where it cracked on its hard landing. There it sat as a new bell was hung in 1872. And when a new church was built in 1900, Selkirk's bell was put into storage in a far, dark basement corner. Its presence faded with every new generation of parishioners and priests.

After being found, it was moved to the legislative building in Winnipeg, then to the Manitoba Archives, and finally, to the St. Boniface Museum—next door to the cathedral where it first rang.

Father J.V. Fyfe points to the original bell commissioned by Lord Selkirk after it was found in the basement of the Roman Catholic Church in St. François Xavier. The church and closer image of the bell are seen in the other images. *BELLS OF THE RED RIVER*, BY MARGARET ARNETT MACLEOD, COPYRIGHT 1937, STOVEL COMPANY LTD., WINNIPEG, MANITOBA

THE FLOWER-BEARING AMERICAN SPY

James Wickes Taylor's mission was distinctly anti-Canadian—to wrest the vast Northwest from the fledgling country and secure it for the United States. But somewhere along the way, the secret agent of the US State Department fell in love with the Red River Settlement and its Métis and French people. As it turned out, the feeling was mutual, and Taylor eventually spent the rest of his life in Winnipeg. He became the US consul in the Manitoba capital and charmed the residents so much that after his death his portrait was hung in city hall. An annual day of commemoration, Crocus Day, was established in his honour.

Portrait of James Wickes Taylor
CITY OF WINNIPEG ARCHIVES

Before he came north to Red River, though, Taylor was an American expansionist, writer and public speaker who spent years advocating for the US to take—through negotiation, military force, or trade—the interior plains north of the 49th parallel. That included the Red River Settlement and lands west along the Saskatchewan Valley.

In 1859, at the request of the governor of Minnesota, Taylor was sent to Red River to investigate the potential for annexation.

Through newspaper articles and meetings with the United States House of Representatives, he touted the agricultural and settlement potential of the Hudson's Bay Company fur-trading territory in the Northwest. Taylor believed the land could support 6-8 million people and make the area from Minnesota north "an Empire in population and resources."

In 1859, at the request of the governor of Minnesota, Taylor was sent to Red River to investigate the potential for annexation. Soon after, he was appointed a special agent of the State Department. He sent back a report in 1860 that recommended the extension of the Reciprocity Treaty of 1854, which had eliminated customs tariffs between the US and British North American provinces and colonies in the east. That treaty led to greater trade between the US and the future provinces of Canada.

Taylor felt a similar agreement in the Northwest would give the US commercial and political advantages without the necessity of forced annexation. He sensed the dissatisfaction of many Red River inhabitants under HBC rule and believed reciprocity was a way in for American interests. Not only could it build commercial ties, but good relations as well. As that resentment with HBC continued to grow, Taylor expected the colonists would naturally turn to the US.

However, reciprocity was soon off the table. The US abolished that arrangement with the eastern British colonies in 1866 in the wake of opposition by American protectionists. After that, Taylor came up with another way to entice the Red River settlers. He proposed the instrument of annexation could be the railway. He felt the future of the isolated Northwest depended on a transcontinental railway and he doubted that Britain was going to build one.

Taylor suggested a line linking the HBC territories with Minnesota, making them dependent on transportation and trade with the US, which would eventually lead the territories into American political and economic orbits. So confident was he of the plan, that he drew up a bill providing for the entry of Red River and the HBC territories into the United States.

But things had drastically changed following the cancellation of the reciprocity treaty.

Firsts in the Northwest 1861-1868

1861

April 5: The first movie in the Red River Settlement is shown. The venue is St. John's Cathedral.

It plays from a magic lantern, a type of image projector into which glass slides are inserted one at a time. The lantern is a gift from Lady Selkirk, Jean Wedderburn-Colville, to the first bishop of Rupert's Land David Anderson.

The slides contain hand-painted images or photographs. A skilled projectionist could move them quickly, making the images appear to move, similar to a flip book.

There is no word on what images were shown. The technology of the magic lantern lasts until the mid-twentieth century when it is superseded by the slide projector.

1862

June 2: Henry McKenney purchases land for a large general store that establishes Winnipeg's now famous intersection of Portage and Main.

Prior to 1862 there were no businesses anywhere along the Main Road between Upper Fort Garry and Point Douglas. The commercial centre in the

Winnipeg's second City Hall (1886-1952).
Exact date of photograph is uncertain.
CITY OF WINNIPEG ARCHIVES

In July 1867, the British North America provinces and colonies in the east merged under Confederation, forming the Dominion of Canada to better protect themselves and the vast territory of Rupert's Land.

In March of that same year, the US purchased Alaska from Russia for $7.2 million. The new Dominion and the British Crown knew the Americans were eyeing Rupert's Land as their next conquest.

The HBC had for years been winding down its fur trading ventures and focusing on retail, leaving the future of its vast territory up in the air. When the HBC decided to sell the land, Britain would not permit the company to sell to the Americans.

The territory was inextricably linked to the Crown. It was King Charles II who had granted the Royal Charter in 1670 that gave the HBC exclusive rights to trade—and to colonize—all the lands that drained into Hudson Bay. The charter was further expanded to the Pacific coast in 1821. The territory was even named after King

area was centred around Upper Fort Garry.

McKenney is ridiculed for his decision as the site is considered by settlers to be undesirable—low lying, muddy and marshy, and covered with scrub oak and poplar. Worst of all, it is a quarter mile from the river, the only source of water. But McKenney proves everyone wrong. The store is a success, and other businesses soon follow. By 1869, thirty-three buildings are clustered around that corner.

McKenney's store is where the first city council of Winnipeg would later meet in a room on the upper floor.

Despite being considered by many to be the founder of Winnipeg, McKenney has been forgotten. No plaques mark the site of The Royal or the store, and no streets bear his name.

1863
December: The first Christmas tree is erected in the Red River Settlement, put on display at Upper Fort Garry a decade before Winnipeg becomes a city.

Christmas festivities took place for many years in the settlement, with dinners and dances at the fort, but that first tree is a new addition—so new that no ornaments exist, according to a December 18, 1915, *Winnipeg Free Press* story.

Shiny tin is collected from the Hudson's Bay Co. shop and a tinsmith requisitioned to create candle holders to attach to the boughs, the story said, noting "ordinary-sized candles used in every household were cut into lengths and fitted into the holders."

The shop is scoured for anything else of ornamental nature. Multi-coloured bead necklaces are found and fastened together to form long chains for garland. Soap is cut into designs and wrapped with tinfoil stripped from gingerbread cakes to make decorations.

1867

August 31: The first billiard table in the West, imported from the eastern US, is installed in George Emmerling's hotel (later the Davis Hotel) on Main between Portage and McDermot in the village of Winnipeg. The table is so popular that Emmerling adds a second in the spring, and the basement of the hotel becomes the Northwest's first billiard saloon.

Charles's cousin, Prince Rupert, who served as the HBC's first governor.

So, two years after Confederation, Canada acquired Rupert's Land for a steal at $1.5 million. The HBC signed the deed of transfer in November 1869, surrendering its territory to the British Crown, which in turn ceded it to Canada. But before Canada could bring the new territory into Confederation, it faced resistance from that little Red River Settlement. And Taylor eyed one last opportunity for annexation.

In December 1869, he was appointed secret agent for the US government, tasked with reporting on the resistance being led by Louis Riel and the terms Riel's provisional government was demanding before they would agree to join Canada. Taylor even followed Riel's delegates to Ottawa and relayed the information on the negotiations back to the US. By May, though, his window of opportunity had closed. After four successive lists of rights were drafted by Riel's provisional government, the final version became the basis for the Manitoba Act, and the creation of Canada's fifth province. It received royal assent on May 12, 1870, and the Act was officially proclaimed on July 15. Taylor watched Canada begin its march west.

In December 1869, he was appointed secret agent for the US government, tasked with reporting on the resistance being led by Louis Riel.

The young country also flipped his plans around. Instead of Taylor wrangling the land for the US, he was hooked by it and converted into a new patriot. Taylor was appointed American consul, based in Winnipeg, in September 1870. It's a post he would hold until his death in 1893. He used the position to plead Riel's case to the American government, advocating for them to intervene in what he considered a breach of faith by the Canadian government. Siding with the Métis, Taylor argued that Canadian authorities promised Riel an amnesty for his role in the 1869-70 resistance yet forced him into exile in the US.

He again sided with the Métis in 1885, when Riel returned to Canada to take part in North-West Resistance in Saskatchewan.

Riel led the Métis in Saskatchewan in asserting their rights, as he had done fifteen years earlier in Manitoba. But the end result was far different. Riel was arrested, put on trial for treason and sentenced to hang. Taylor tried to convince the US government it had a duty toward Riel, who had become an American citizen in 1883 while in exile. His efforts to back the Métis led to beatings at the hands of Canadian troops, who arrived in Red River from Ontario after Manitoba joined Confederation. They were sent to oversee the transfer of authority to the Canadian government, but many of them had looked forward to confronting Riel and his supporters in retaliation for the death of Ontario Orangeman Thomas Scott.

Despite being a target of the troops, Taylor consistently voiced his support of the French and Métis and reported that "flagrant and cowardly" assaults against them, perpetuated by the troops, were a daily occurrence.

"So far this incident has tended to identify me with this long-suffering population, I do not regret it," he wrote.

However, Taylor seemed at times to play both sides. It was on his recommendation, during the 1885 resistance, that an American force patrolled the international border to prevent aid from reaching Riel and his men. And despite his declared love for his adopted land, some of his correspondences with the US government refer to his stay as an "exile" and a "foreign residence."

Drawing of James Wickes Taylor

MANITOBA FREE PRESS, MAY 29, 1892. MANITOBA LEGISLATIVE LIBRARY, BIOGRAPHICAL SCRAPBOOK B1, PAGE 103

Still, Taylor was one of, if not the first person, to alert Lieutenant-Governor Adams George Archibald of an impending Fenian attack on Manitoba. The raids were a series of incursions carried out by the Fenian Brotherhood, a US-based Irish republican organization, on military fortifications, customs posts and other targets in Canada.

The raids were an attempt to pressure the British to withdraw from Ireland, but they didn't achieve their aims. In fact, they were sometimes farcical. In one instance, about thirty-five men captured an HBC post and customs house they believed were in Manitoba, just north of the international border. But they were actually about three kilometres south of it, in the Dakota Territory of Pembina. Prior to the Treaty of 1818, in which the 49th parallel was agreed upon as the international boundary, Pembina was in Rupert's Land. The treaty transferred the Red River Valley south of the boundary to the US. Apparently the Fenian Brotherhood hadn't brushed up on their geography. The would-be raiders were arrested by the US Cavalry without ever getting into Manitoba, in part thanks to Taylor's tip.

It was also thanks to Taylor that Manitoba's population experienced a significant bump. He obtained bonding regulations from the American Treasury Department in 1871 to facilitate the movement of immigrants through the US into Manitoba.

As the province grew and the threats of the Ontario soldiers vanished, Taylor was embraced by Manitoba. His efforts in promoting the province were hailed by many. His past hopes for annexation with the US were either overlooked or forgotten.

Taylor's reputation for the remainder of his life was that of a charming, genial, and courteous gentleman. He developed a custom of picking crocuses, the early blooming flower of the Prairies, and presenting them to ladies.

"Nothing endeared the consul to the homes of the people more than this simple act of thoughtfulness, back of which was the desire to give a cheering message to people who had been shut in much during the long cold winter of the region," the *Winnipeg Evening Tribune* wrote in a November 1924 story.

Taylor was embraced by Manitoba. His past hopes for annexation with the US were either overlooked or forgotten.

Not only were the crocus presentations a common anecdotal story among Winnipeggers, but they were also well documented by Taylor. When his executors went through his papers following his death, they found a detailed list of five hundred ladies who had received crocus bouquets.

Interior of old city hall, showing the council chambers and the portrait of James Wickes Taylor hanging on second floor, above the mayor's chair. CITY OF WINNIPEG ARCHIVES

When Taylor died on April 28, 1893, Queen Victoria instructed staff to lower the British flag to half-mast at Windsor Castle. In Winnipeg, one newspaper wrote a glowing obituary: "So closely … had Consul Taylor been identified with the history and development of our country, and so earnest a friend did he prove himself of it, that he attracted to himself an amount of respect and genuine love on the part of the public which few men ever accumulate even in their own land," the piece declared, according to *The Dictionary of Canadian Biography.*

William Coldwell, parliamentary reporter for the *Manitoba Free Press,* wrote "in his own delightful, quiet, unobtrusive way, Consul Taylor was one of the few real heroes of the Canadian Northwest."

The city of Winnipeg commissioned a full-length portrait of Taylor holding a bouquet of crocuses and hung it in the main corridor at the old gingerbread city hall, alongside the portraits honouring the past and present mayors. It was later moved to the council chambers, where it hung on a wall over the gallery, directly above the mayor's chair.

In the painting, Taylor is standing next to a table where he has just laid down a bundle of crocuses. For many years, April 28 was known as Crocus Day, and it became custom to pick crocuses and place them in front of the portrait as a token of remembrance and affection. The prairie crocus was eventually adopted as Manitoba's floral emblem in 1906.

Whether he wanted to or not, Taylor eventually returned to the States. He is buried in Utica, New York.

"In his own delightful, quiet, unobtrusive way, Consul Taylor was one of the few real heroes of the Canadian Northwest." William Coldwell

The two City of Winnipeg crests. The one at left was used from 1874–1973 and featured a bison, locomotive, and sheaves of wheat. The motto was "commerce, prudence, industry." The second, and current one (at right), was adopted in 1973 following the amalgamation of Winnipeg's municipalities. It features the crocus, the Fort Garry Gate and stars symbolizing the 13 municipal governments unified to create the new city. The motto is "one with the strength of many." CITY OF WINNIPEG

REPUBLIC OF MANITOBAH

Louis Riel is synonymous with Manitoba, regarded as its founder and the one who proposed the name for Canada's first western province. But credit for the name isn't his alone.

Thomas Spence, before anyone else, penned the province's future name—as Manitobah—in reference to the large lake and surrounding territory. His name was an anglicized version of that used by Indigenous people to refer to the great spirit Manitou, believed to inhabit the waters.

Images from the National Film Board
of Canada's 1978 animated vignette,
Spence's Republic NATIONAL FILM BOARD
OF CANADA (NFB)

In stormy weather, waves crashing against the limestone rocks of offshore islands in the narrows—the slim channel between the northern and southern parts of Lake Manitoba—resounded eerily. First Nations people believed the sound was that of a drum pounded by Manitou. The Cree referred to the narrows as Manitouwapow, which means the strait of Manitou. To the Ojibwa, it was Manidoobaa or Manito-bau, which held the same meaning.

Thomas Spence PROVINCIAL ARCHIVES OF MANITOBA, LEGISLATIVE COUNCIL 1870, N16739

European explorers, traders and settlers were introduced to Indigenous names and legends that had been held in oral tradition for generations. When the Europeans attempted to write the vernacular, it led to a blend of languages. Cartographer and founding member of the North-West Company of fur traders Peter Pond named the lake on a 1785 map as Lake Minnitopa and on another as Lake Minnetopar.

Others simply disregarded the Indigenous name—and creativity—altogether. French explorer Pierre Gaultier de Varennes et de La Vérendrye, in 1738, gave the body of water the unvarnished name of Lac des Prairies, or Lake of the Prairies.

Spence gets credit for first writing Manito-bau down as Manitobah, the closest version of the name we now know.

Despite his substantial contribution, he's more likely remembered as a caricature than a key historical figure. Spence led a failed, almost comical, short-lived provisional government. His attempt fell flat, but just two years later Riel did much the same thing and became the founder of the province. Consequently, Spence's venture is almost forgotten in the birth story of Manitoba.

Born in Edinburgh, Scotland in 1832, he moved to Lower Canada (Quebec) in 1852 and headed west in 1866 to the Red River Settlement around Upper Fort Garry. It was a year before the new Dominion of Canada was established through the confederation of the British colonies of New Brunswick, Nova Scotia, Upper Canada (Ontario), and Lower Canada. The impending union was on the minds and mouths of many in the fledgling settlement of Red River. The new dominion ended at the Great Lakes, and west of that was the vast fur-trading territory of the Hudson's Bay Company, known as Rupert's Land.

Red River was in the middle of that remote fur-trading land and close to the international border, where settlement was advancing west in the United States. Recognizing the unfolding change—even the HBC was well into winding down its fur trading ventures and focusing on retail—some folks in Red River began to lobby to join the new Canada. But others pushed for annexation to the US.

Spence was one of those who quickly raised the torch for the pro-Canadian cause. In December 1866 he advertised a public meeting to be held in the courthouse at Upper Fort Garry. The aim was

Firsts in the Northwest 1871-1876

1871

The port of Emerson is established as the first land border customs station in Canada, eight years before the town of Emerson is incorporated.

Though no longer active, the original customs building in Emerson still stands today. It is a log house constructed in 1868 and it is alleged that Louis Riel stopped there for the night when he was leaving Manitoba in 1870 to escape the approaching expeditionary force from Ontario.

Map shows Emerson Branch of the Canadian Pacific Railway in 1887.
PROVINCIAL ARCHIVES OF MANITOBA

Over one million travellers are now processed at the Emerson border crossing each year, making it the second busiest along the Canada-United States border west of the Great Lakes, behind only the Pacific Highway Border Crossing between British Columbia and Washington state.

February 18: The first unofficial tonsorial artist—a barber—starts up in a rented room above Monchamp's Saloon on Post Office Street in the Red River Settlement. A member of the Ontario Rifles, he offers shaves and haircuts when not on duty.

The Rifles were part of the 1870 Red River Expedition sent from Ontario to confront Louis Riel and oversee the transfer of the settlement from Riel's provisional government to the Canadian government. Many stayed and settled in the area. The first advertised barber in the area was W. Wood Fairweather, who opened a shop in the Davis Hotel on the Main Road in 1872.

April 14: The Northwest's first baker opens at the corner of Rorie Street and Owen Street (now McDermot Avenue) in the Red River Settlement, selling a two-pound loaf for six cents.

April 19: Meteorological observations begin for the area that would become Winnipeg.

June 4: The first boot and shoe merchant in the Northwest, William Wellband, opens a shop on Main Street, near Notre Dame Avenue.

September 1: The first veterinary practice is opened in the Northwest by William Forbes Alloway.

He later opens the first tobacco shop and the first private bank as well. A wealthy man, Alloway later provides $100,000 to help establish The Winnipeg Foundation, the first community foundation in Canada, in 1921.

When he dies in 1930, his entire estate is left to the foundation, making his total contribution about $2 million. The foundation continues to be one of the largest of its kind in North America.

September 11: The first stagecoach in the Northwest rattles and bumps along the rutted dirt of Main Road and clatters to a halt in front of the Davis Hotel, heralding a major milestone for the soon-to-be city of Winnipeg.

It is the most significant transportation advancement since the first steamboat pulled up in 1859. The stage, with its southern terminus in Minnesota, means Manitobans

to pass a resolution to request Britain permit the Red River Settlement to join the confederation. The new dominion had gained some legislative powers but remained under the sovereignty of the British monarch (until the Constitution Act in 1982).

A pro-American group led by hotelier George Emmerling intended to oppose the resolution. Spence got wind of that, so he and four friends gathered early and passed it. They then decided, probably without much consideration, to go to Emmerling's bar on Main Street to celebrate.

Halfway there they met Emmerling and his opposition group, along with others from the pro-Canada group who were unaware an earlier meeting had taken place. Everyone pressured Spence to return to the courthouse where a second meeting was held. It erupted into chaos with everyone shouting and arguing and, at one point, an angry Emmerling trying to collect on an outstanding tab from one of his bar customers. Tempers flared, fists flew, and the meeting became a brawl. It spilled outside where the frigid December air persuaded everyone to go into Emmerling's bar, where the hostilities continued.

The fighting eventually waned after most of the bar's contents were destroyed. By the time the mess was mopped up, nothing had changed.

The fighting eventually waned after most of the bar's contents were destroyed. By the time the mess was mopped up, nothing had changed. No consensus was reached, and the meeting was nothing more than bedlam.

Consequently, the original passing of the resolution stood, at least in Spence's mind. And the settlement's newspaper, the *Nor'Wester*, reported

can reach the St. Paul-Minnesota Railway—and thereby the rest of the continental US—at any time of year. All they have to do is endure five days of shaking and discomfort.

October 30: The first public school in the Northwest opens with thirty-five students and William Fisher (W. F.) Luxton as teacher.

The 20-by-18-foot log building is on land donated by William Gomez de Fonseca at the southeast corner of Maple Street and Common Street (now Henry Avenue) in the Red River Settlement. The

Winnipeg's first school, circa 1909 *THE WINNIPEG TRIBUNE, NOV. 11, 1933, P13*

as much, publishing the resolution without any mention of the underhanded early meeting or the few participants. It also described the second meeting as a disorderly group discussing matters which had no bearing on the resolution. It's not clear what happened to the resolution, if it was ever sent and what response the British Crown offered.

In 1867, Spence moved to Portage la Prairie where he opened a store and again turned his attention to politics. He felt the community, about 85 kilometres west of Upper Fort Garry, had grown to the point where it needed political organization. There were about four hundred people but no courts, no police, no taxation, and no government. The community was outside the jurisdiction of the Council of Assiniboia, which oversaw the Red River Settlement and whose powers extended only 80 kilometres west of Fort Garry. It was a blank slate for Spence and his big ambitions.

In June 1867 he pulled together some of the settlers and hosted a meeting in his store, where he laid out a plan to set up a government and appeal to Britain to grant legal powers and protection.

He apparently overlooked, or simply ignored, the fact he was laying claim to territory still under HBC jurisdiction—Rupert's Land didn't become part of an expanded Canada until 1870—never mind the fact the Indigenous people were never consulted or considered in any of it.

Spence sent his request to the Crown, but no reply came. By early 1868, he and his supporters decided to just push forward and instead organize as a republic with a president rather than a monarch. Spence became president and named the domain New Caledonia, after his homeland. Caledonia was the Latin name used by the Roman Empire to refer to the part of Great Britain north of the River Forth, which includes most of the land area of Scotland. Today, it is more commonly used as an affectionate name for all of Scotland.

Shortly afterwards, though, Spence had a change of heart and renamed the district Republic of Manitobah, after the lake with the spirit in

building, with a thatched straw roof, had previously been used as a store and living quarters.

Luxton would go on to found the *Manitoba Free Press* in partnership with John A. Kenny the following year, with the first issue on November 9, 1872.

November 20: The Northwest's first telegraph is sent from Fort Garry on the same day the line is completed.

It is sent by Adams George Archibald, lieutenant governor of Manitoba and the North-West Territories, to the governor general in Ottawa: "We may now count in hours the work that used to occupy weeks," part of Archibald's message reads.

1872
May 9: The first cab for hire is sent out into the muddy streets of what would become Winnipeg. The horse-drawn wagon, owned by David Landrigan, is stationed at a stand in front of the Davis Hotel.

1873
March 6: The first streetlamp west of the Great Lakes is erected in Winnipeg outside the Davis Hotel on the west side of Main Road, a half block from Portage Avenue. The arc light uses an inert

Lake Manitoba Narrows commemorative
monument GORDON GOLDSBOROUGH

the narrows. In February 1868, he and his new
council sent another letter overseas, to the British
Colonial Office in London, informing it of the
new entity and body politic. In a way, Portage la
Prairie was the first capital of Manitoba(h).

In a January 1868 letter to the Canadian
Parliament, mirroring the one sent to the British
Colonial Office, Spence outlined the territory
as extending from the US border north to Lake
Manitoba and "as far as Manitoba house," a
fur-trading post on the western shore of the lake,
south of the narrows. The eastern edge bordered
the District of Assiniboia, and the western border
was the Souris River and Little Saskatchewan
River—approximately the 100th meridian.

Needing revenue to build the structures for his
government, such as a council house, courthouse
and jail, Spence set out to raise the money by
imposing a tariff on imports. Notices were served
on all traders in the area, but the regulations were
disregarded by most. The HBC officer in Portage,
for example, refused to pay or acknowledge
Spence's administration.

gas and is illuminated for the first time on March 12, six years before inventor Thomas Edison's incandescent bulb is created.

April 24: The first house-to-house water service is established in Winnipeg by George Rath. He builds a tank on a wooden cart, pulled by an oxen team, and uses a pump and forty-foot hose to deliver water to the door, eliminating the need for multiple trips with pails.

May 3: Toothaches meet their match when the Northwest's first dentist, J.W. Barstow, opens in the Davis Hotel on Main Road in a part of the Red River Colony that had become known as Winnipeg.

Winnipeg Water Works ox cart, 1875, prior to George Rath creating his home delivery service CITY OF WINNIPEG ARCHIVES A569

May 4: The first two rats ever reported in Canada arrive in Winnipeg. They were stowaways in a package of goods on a steamboat.

August: The first soda fountain in the West is opened by Dr. Curtis James Bird, the speaker of the legislative assembly. It is located inside his drug store, Apothecaries' Hall, at the corner of Main Road and Bannatyne Street (later Main Street and Bannatyne Avenue) in Winnipeg.

November 3: The first 150 recruits of the North-West Mounted Police, forerunner to the RCMP, gather at Lower Fort Garry to start training. The new national police force was created through an act of Parliament on May 23, 1873, and became official on August 30.

1874
January 4: The first fruit from California arrives in Northwest. It comes to Winnipeg via Moorehead, Minnesota, in a covered caravan. There's no record of the type of fruit.

February 19: Winnipeg's first police force debuts, taking over from a provincial force.
The first chief is John Ingram, who is forced to resign in July 1875 when

his own constables find him during a raid of a bordello in the city's red-light district. He moves to Calgary where he becomes police chief.

Chief Constable John S. Ingram

June 19: The first murder is committed in Winnipeg, just months after it is incorporated as a city on November 8, 1873.

James R. Brown is left lying on the dirt in the middle of the Portage Trail, about a block from Main Road in the dark, early hours after the saloons have closed. His body is found to have more than thirty stab and slash wounds, including to the throat, lungs, and through the skull into the brain.

Joseph Michaud, a 23-year-old soldier from

There wasn't much Spence could do without a court or jail to give weight to his authority. His power faced its biggest test when local shoemaker Angus MacPherson accused Spence and his cronies of using the money from the levies to buy themselves booze rather than for the improvement of the colony.

MacPherson was warned, like the HBC officer, that once the institutions were in place to enforce the rules, he would face consequences if he continued to flout them. Not only did MacPherson ignore the threat, but he also repeated his accusations and urged others to refuse payment until a strict accounting of government income and expenditure was made public by an independent audit.

Spence needed to take a stand or risk his authority being completely undermined. It was his biggest test to prove he could govern and enforce the rules. And he failed. He issued an arrest warrant for MacPherson with a charge of treason. The republic's entire police force—two men—were dispatched to bring him in. As there was still no jail, it was decided the matter would go straight to a trial inside the home of one of the constables.

Giving credence to MacPherson's claim, the two officers were drunk when they headed out to make the arrest. And they were noisy. The bells on their sleigh rang out while the constables allegedly bellowed and sang about their mission to seize "this here lawbreaker."

Spence needed to take a stand or risk his authority being completely undermined.

MacPherson heard them as they approached his house, so he ran, hoping to reach the boundary of Assiniboia, beyond the republic's alleged jurisdiction. But the constables easily caught up and captured him.

John McLean, a fellow Scotsman and a Portage la Prairie-area farmer, was on his way home when the constables' sleigh approached from

Winnipeg in 1873, the year of James Brown's murder
PROVINCIAL ARCHIVES OF MANITOBA, WINNIPEG-STREETS-MAIN

Quebec, who came to the city as part of the Wolseley expedition, is arrested and charged the next day.

July 8: The NWMP, now numbering close to three hundred members, sets out on its famous March West to establish detachments in the 200,000 square miles of new territory under Canada's command.

Starting from Fort Dufferin, just north of Emerson, they begin the trek on horseback, accompanied by a long line of Red River carts and Métis drivers.

July 16: Inside the St. James Restaurant in

Winnipeg, a meeting takes place to establish the first private social club for men in western Canada. The Manitoba Club is incorporated the next month.

It is another 98 years before the first Jewish members are allowed and 117 years after its founding before women are admitted in 1991.

Now Canada's oldest operating private club, it has been visited by princes, prime ministers, Mark Twain, and American Civil War General William Tecumseh Sherman.

July 31: The first Mennonites—65 families—arrive at The Forks in Winnipeg by steamer from Grand Forks.

The sternwheeler *International* docks at the HBC warehouse, at The Forks, in 1874, carrying a group of early Mennonite settlers. Upper Fort Garry can be seen at top left. *THE WINNIPEG TRIBUNE*, MAY 12, 1952, P5

the opposite direction. MacPherson jumped out and dashed over, pleading for McLean to help. McLean stood between MacPherson and the constables, demanding the offers stand back.

Once the situation was explained, McLean advised MacPherson to go with the constables but vowed to attend the trial. McLean then rushed home, where he had three friends visiting, and all four made their way into the village for the evening trial.

MacPherson was seated at a long table. Spence was at the end, flanked by the constables and a brother of one of the officers. Spence, acting as judge, also assumed the role of plaintiff. That didn't sit well with McLean, who barked out in his thick brogue, "Y'canna act as judge and accuser baith!" according to *Extraordinary Tales from Manitoba History*, written by James Warren Chafe.

The constables snarled back, and McLean, not one to retreat, moved closer to them. And once again, a meeting led by Spence erupted in punches. A lamp was knocked over during the fracas, leaving people swinging wildly in the dark, not knowing who they were hitting. It ended in an explosion of gunfire when McLean's friends pulled out revolvers and fired into the ceiling. And then silence.

Spence had taken shelter under a table from where he pleaded, "For God's sake man, don't shoot! I have a wife and family!"

The experiment known as the Republic of Manitobah was effectively over. Spence had earlier been advised by the Governor of Rupert's Land that his bogus government held no authority. That was reiterated on May 30, 1868, when Spence received a letter with a similar response from the British Colonial Office.

"The creation of a separate government in the manner set forth in these papers has no force in law, and that they have no authority to create or organize government, or even to set up municipal institutions for themselves," it stated.

His republic may have collapsed but Spence left his stamp on what became a postage-sized province just two years later.

After Manitobah's failure, he moved to the shores of the lake he named and briefly worked

August 26: The first execution in western Canada (after transfer of Rupert's Land from HBC) is the hanging in Winnipeg of Joseph Michaud for killing James R. Brown in June.

September 17: The first municipal tax paid by anyone in the Northwest is handed to the city collector in Winnipeg by William Dodd. The amount is $4.

September 29: The first patent in Manitoba is granted. It's for a pipe wrench, designed by James Bedman, which makes tweaks on the world's first such wrench. That first one, known as

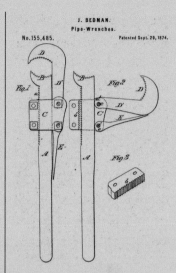

James Bedman pipe wrench patent application CHRISTIAN CASSIDY, WEST END DUMPLINGS

the Stillson wrench, was patented in 1869 in the US, itself an improvement on the monkey wrench, first invented in 1858.

The upper jaw on Bedman's version hinges

back for larger pipes. It is also curved to better fit that shape. Bedman's tool also has a serrated handle section to lock the jaw, eliminating the adjusting nut used by Stillson.

Unfortunately, Bedman doesn't get to see his invention put into wide use. He dies in late 1874 or early 1875 at age 42. The date is not certain because obituaries often took a while to appear in the newspaper and his was posted in February 1875.

Winnipeg historian Christian Cassidy, in his *West End Dumplings* blog, notes that no further references to Bedman's wrench can be found after Bedman's death "so his invention may have died with him."

1875
May 5: The first mention is made in the *Winnipeg Free Press* of a bicycle in the city, which would make it the first one in the entire Northwest.

The world's first pedal-driven bicycle—or velocipede—was invented in early 1864 by Pierre Michaux and his son Ernest in France. In 1866, one of their workers emigrated to the United States and patented the bicycle there, calling it the bone-shaker.

June 14: The first pipe organ in the Northwest arrives on a steamboat from Moorhead, North Dakota, and is installed in St. Boniface Cathedral, across the Red River from Winnipeg.

It stands six metres tall, four metres wide and three deep, and weighs nearly 5,500 kilograms. The unloading takes more than fifty men.

October 11: The first Icelanders arrive in Winnipeg—285 people.

Exactly one week later they set out to establish a new community on the west shore of Lake Winnipeg, starting the nucleus of what Gimli, named after the home of the gods in Norse mythology.

Some 1,200 settlers join them the next year and set the foundation for what is now the largest Icelandic settlement outside of Iceland.

1876
August 15: The first sailboat race in the West takes place between employees of the Red River Transportation Company and federal government employees. The wager is $20. There's no report on who wins.

to extract salt. He was back in the Red River Settlement by 1869, just as Canada was taking over Rupert's Land and looking to expand its footprint in the West.

The script he wrote was being acted upon by another cast. Riel was leading a provisional government in the Red River area and had established a list of rights in November 1869 that it considered as necessary conditions for the territory to join Confederation.

Spence was initially arrested by Riel's forces because of his prior association with John Christian Schultz. During Spence's 1866 push for Confederation in Red River, he became friends with Schultz, whose newspaper, the *Nor'Wester,* advocated for the end of HBC rule in Red River and annexation with Canada.

By 1869, Schultz had sold the paper and was the leader of a group of expansionists known as the Canadian Party. They fiercely defied Riel's government and encouraged anglophone/Protestant immigration from Ontario, fueling worry among the Métis about the loss of their culture and lands.

In his journal, written during the tumultuous, defining years of the Red River in 1869-70, Alexander Begg—local merchant and founding member of the Manitoba Historical Society—wrote that Spence was taken prisoner in 1870 on suspicion of carrying letters between persons opposed to Riel. But just eleven days after his arrest, Spence was appointed editor of Riel's newspaper, *The New Nation*. Spence also joined Riel's council and brought along the name of his failed republic.

During negotiations for the transfer of Red River to the Government of Canada, Riel had promoted a different name for the new province. When the second version of the list of rights was being drawn up in January 1870, there was no name listed for the proposed province. The Red River Settlement and District of Assiniboia were each referred to by name, and each as a territory.

By the time the third list was written in March, Riel pushed for the region to be a single province and a resolution was passed that it be "known as the Province of Assiniboia." Even his administration had become known as the Provisional

October 13: The West's first chimney sweep brushes into action, prompted by poor reports from Winnipeg's fire inspector of stovepipes.

November 5: The founding meeting is held for the Manitoba Curling Club, the first such club in the Northwest.

Nearly seventy members are signed up and the rink is built on Andrew Bannatyne's property (present site of Victoria-Albert School, west of the Exchange District in Winnipeg).

Eight members play the first club game on December 11, in a contest where the prize is a barrel of oatmeal to be donated to the General Hospital. The *Manitoba Free Press* reports it as the first game of curling ever played in the province, but it is more accurate to call it the first club-organized game.

Curlers have been meeting on the frozen river since the 1860s. According to the *Curling Capital: Winnipeg and the Roarin' Game, 1876 to 1988*, workers at Stony Mountain

Penitentiary converted a woodshed into a one-sheet rink in 1873-74. The rocks they used, as did the curling club, were made from iron, which was readily available, as opposed to expensive granite stones that had to be imported from Scotland.

The Manitoba Curling Club's first-ever bonspiel is held December 16, 1876, when the Manitoba Curling Club rink is formally opened. It proves so popular that gas lanterns are added in January 1877 so games can be played into the evening.

In 1880, a rift arises when several members want to switch to granite rocks. They split away and form the aptly named Granite Curling Club.

The Granite's first games are played in 1881, on sheets of ice beneath a canvas tent on Post Office Street (now Lombard Avenue). As interest wanes in the iron rocks, the Manitoba Curling Club folds in 1883. The Granite remains the oldest curling club in Western Canada.

Government of Assiniboia. But when his council delegates were sent to Ottawa, carrying that list of rights, Riel had a change of mind.

On April 19, 1870, he sent a letter of instructions to his delegate, Father Noël-Joseph Ritchot: "The name of the country is already written in all hearts, that of Red River. Fancy delights in that of Manitoba, but the situation seems to demand that of North-West. Friends of the old government are pleased with that of Assiniboia (but) it is not generally-enough liked to be kept. Choose one of the two names Manitoba or North-West."

The federal legislation providing for the admission of the Red River region as Canada's fifth province received royal assent and became law on May 12, 1870. The Parliament of Canada passed the Manitoba Act on July 15, 1870, officially establishing the new province, the boundaries of which were just west enough to include Portage la Prairie.

Sir John A. Macdonald, in announcing it, said the Manitoba name was selected for its pleasant sound and association with the original inhabitants.

Spence's own republic may have lasted less than a year, but the name he first wrote will forever endure—minus the H.

Sir John A. Macdonald, in announcing it, said the Manitoba name was selected for its pleasant sound and association with the original inhabitants.

Still, there is a vestige, or perhaps more of a small tribute, to his original efforts. Tucked into the southeast edge of Portage la Prairie is the Republic of Manitobah Park, a seventy-acre greenspace with multiple sports fields—and an H.

THE MAN WHO SAVED THE BISON

A decision by a young Manitoban more than 150 years ago helped change the seemingly doomed course of one of Canada's greatest symbols of the Prairies.

Many of the bison seen today in Winnipeg's Assiniboine Park Zoo, as well as zoos and parks around the world, are direct descendants of those rescued by Charles Valentine Alloway from the slaughters that took place during early settlement.

Bison at Lake Audy, Riding Mountain National Park DARREN BERNHARDT

At one time during the nineteenth century, bison numbers were estimated to be as high as 60 million, a thunderous mass across the Canadian Prairies and US Great Plains between the Missouri and Saskatchewan rivers. European explorers wrote about the ground being obscured by a dark horde reaching as far as the curve of land at the horizon. As late as 1870, missionaries in Canada reported seeing herds numbering a half million. But by 1888, no wild bison were left in Canada and only one herd remained in the wild in the United States, in Yellowstone National Park.

It was the foresight of Alloway that ensured bison didn't become an historical footnote. His efforts mean that the largest land mammal in North America still exists, casting an imposing, almost-prehistoric contour where it roams.

Alloway was twenty-three years old in 1873 when he recognized that the bison hunt was changing. He hunted and traded with the First Nations and Métis, but finding the herds required more distant treks west of the Red River Valley and the newly incorporated city of Winnipeg, where he lived, even well beyond Portage la Prairie.

Charles Valentine Alloway
THE WINNIPEG EVENING TRIBUNE,
JUNE 24, 1925 P13

"I conceived the idea that the day was dawning when the vast herds would be depleted," he told *The Winnipeg Tribune* in 1929, four years before his death.

Alloway recalled how he had once bought some 21,000 buffalo hides

European explorers wrote about the ground being obscured by a dark horde reaching as far as the curve of land at the horizon.

from a single brigade of hunters, paying $3 for the average-sized and $4 for the large ones.

"It didn't take any higher mathematics to realize this rate of killing them off couldn't go on forever, especially as there were dozens of brigades out hunting at a time."

But there were few like him who paid any particular attention to what was happening.

Slaughter of Buffalo on the Kansas Pacific Railroad REPRODUCED FROM *THE PLAINS OF THE GREAT WEST*, BY COL. R. I. DODGE/ WHYTE MUSEUM OF THE CANADIAN ROCKIES

"We took our buffaloes and buffalo skins and pemmican as we now take our rain and crops as a matter of course, something that always had been and, presumably, always would be," Alloway said in that 1929 *Tribune* interview.

But at some point, after recognizing the impact the hunts—and his own support of them through his buying of hides—were having, Alloway made

a decision that would alter the cascading course of the bison.

In spring 1873, he and James McKay—a Métis fur trader and member of the Manitoba Legislative Council—joined a hunting group of

Gathering Buffalo Bones on the Prairie Alberta, Canada

Bison bones gathered in Alberta and piled alongside the rail line. Date unknown.

Métis near Battleford, Saskatchewan. The hunting brigade was out for hides as well as meat for pemmican, but the motivation for Alloway and McKay was preservation of the prairie beasts, where possible.

McKay was fluent in multiple Indigenous languages and someone with a thorough knowledge of the Prairies, having been born and raised on them. He was also an advisor, interpreter, and negotiator of Treaties 1-4, and assisted as commissioner or

James McKay in 1873
PROVINCIAL ARCHIVES OF MANITOBA

William Forbes Alloway, circa 1925
PROVINCIAL ARCHIVES OF MANITOBA

co-commissioner in Treaties 5 and 6. He found equal comfort and success in hunting and trading as he did in politics, helping to bridge the gap between the old West and new as the region's evolution from frontier to settled lands took hold and Red River society grew more complex.

Alloway was born in Ireland and raised in the bustling urban areas of Hamilton and Montreal after his parents emigrated to Upper Canada. He arrived in Manitoba in 1870, along with his younger brother, William, as part of the Wolseley expedition—the military force sent to Red River to oversee the transfer of political control from Louis Riel's provisional government to Canada.

William, an intellectual, pursued various professions such as a veterinarian, tobacconist, horse auctioneer, foreman for McKay's freighter business, politician, speculator in Métis scrip and eventually, a millionaire banker. He made his first significant sum of money through the resale of horses and

Firsts in the Northwest 1877-1888

1877

October 8: The bells of St. Boniface Cathedral lead a chorus that includes whistles from nearby mills, musical bands, artillery salutes, and cheers from crowds lining the riverbank, as the first locomotive arrives in the Canadian west.

The Countess of Dufferin launches the railroad era west of the Great Lakes and helps connect the entire country. Built in 1872, it is used in Minnesota and the Dakota Territory until 1877 when it is sold to Joseph Whitehead, a contractor for the Canadian Pacific

Countess of Dufferin, taken some time between 1877 and 1910
PASTFORWARD WINNIPEG PUBLIC LIBRARY, WP0708

Railway. He names it after Hariot Georgina Hamilton-Temple-Blackwood, Countess of Dufferin, the wife of the Earl of Dufferin, the third Governor General of Canada.

The couple was visiting the area a few days before the engine arrived in Winnipeg and were given the honour of driving the first spike for what would become the CPR's Pembina branch line—the first railway in Western Canada.

November 23: The first telephone in the Northwest is installed in the Winnipeg home of Horace McDougall, less than two years after Alexander Graham Bell received his patent for the device in March 1876.

McDougall is manager of the Northwestern Telegraph Company and rents the first set of telephones—one for his home and one for the office, both at 152 Garry St. He obtains a licence as the sole agent to install and make use of the Bell patent in western Canada

In fall 1880, McDougall sells his interests to the new Bell Telephone Company of Canada.

carts to Canadian Pacific Railway surveying parties. He used it as capital to co-found Alloway and Champion Bank, which eventually became the largest private banking firm in Canada.

In 1921, he established Canada's first community foundation, The Winnipeg Foundation, with a gift of $100,000. The philanthropic organization still exists and oversees more than 3,700 endowment funds. In 2022 alone, it distributed $85 million to the community.

Meanwhile, Charles Alloway was more adventure-minded and content roaming the Prairies. He was fascinated with bison and their sheer size—both individually, and as herds that blanketed the land and shook the ground. The bulls can stand as high as seven feet tall at the hump, measure 10-12 feet from nose to tail, and weigh as much as 2,200 pounds. The cows are a bit slighter, weighing closer to 1,000 pounds and standing about five feet at the hump. Calves can weigh as much as 70 pounds when born.

In a 1972 story in *Wild West* magazine, Alloway recalled a trip to Saskatchewan's Qu'Appelle Valley and how his party one day was advised by Indigenous hunters to quickly abandon their camp. Moments later the site and land around it was flattened by a "brown river of buffalo." A herd estimated by Alloway at more than a million rushed through "at the rate of about 10 a second."

The experience left as strong an impact on Alloway's psyche as it did on his campsite. So when the numbers of bison were in clear decline, he stepped up.

Which brings us back to that spring 1873 excursion with McKay and the Métis.

[Alloway] was fascinated with bison and their sheer size— both individually, and as herds that blanketed the land and shook the ground.

SPRING 1873 HUNT

Alloway brought along an ox cart and rescued three bison calves—two bulls and a heifer—orphaned after the mothers were shot. He and McKay hired one of the Métis men to go to Prince Albert and buy a domestic cow, whose milk was used to feed and sustain the calves.

Postcard showing Deer Lodge at Silver Heights, circa 1871-74, when it was owned by Donald Smith PROVINCIAL ARCHIVES OF MANITOBA

The animals were kept in a thirty-acre enclosure at Deer Lodge, the name for McKay's property north of today's Assiniboine Park in Winnipeg. The site is now an entire neighbourhood, and home to Deer Lodge Centre, a long-term care facility on Portage Avenue.

"They really did well, once they got used to our domestic cow. The cow raised the three of them," Alloway said in the 1929 *Tribune* article.

Alloway and McKay joined the spring hunt again the following year. The brigades typically consisted of 80-100 hunters, their wives, and their families—in all, perhaps 2,000 people, Alloway recalled.

"We did not come up with the buffaloes until sometime in May and then they were west of Milk River, halfway between Regina and Moose Jaw, and near the International border," he said. "This time we also got three calves, one bull, and a heifer." The bull became sick and died but "the foundation for our buffalo herd was laid," Alloway said.

Postcard, circa 1905, with the caption: Buffalo at Deer Lodge COURTESY
DARREN BERHARDT

The herd was expanded in 1877 when Alloway
sent out a hunter who brought back thirty of the
animals from just south of the Pembina Hills, the
escarpment that runs from Manitoba to South
Dakota and forms the western wall of the Red
River Valley. A number of them had shown up
again in the region.

By 1878 the Alloway herd had grown from five
calves to thirteen.

1878

February 3: The first pawn-broker opens, located on Main Street in Winnipeg, on the site of what is now the Confederation Life Building.

February 5: The first thrift store, Mrs. Finney's, opens on Notre Dame Street (now Notre Dame Avenue) near Portage and Main in Winnipeg.

May 27: Seven students take the first-ever exams at the University of Manitoba.

The first U of M graduate is William Reginald Gunn, on June 9, 1880, with a Bachelor of Arts degree and honours in Natural Sciences.

June 22: The first circus troupe visits Manitoba—and goes bankrupt.

Dr. Hager's Paris Circus (from Michigan, not Paris) pulls into Winnipeg on June 21 and holds its first show on the 22nd.

After a long and seemingly successful run, which the Manitoba Free Press said drew in large crowds each day, the proprietor and his son-in-law duck out of town on July 5 and leave the performers "dead broke and more than a 1,000 miles from home."

The paper said the financial troubles started earlier,

as the troupe travelled by horse-and-cart and boat, from town to town. The performers went mostly unpaid and were fed crackers and lies, according to the *Free Press*.

The owner would routinely tell them he was paying off loans and transport costs and promise that the next stop would be the big payday.

Despite their situation, the stranded performers arrange a show at city hall with half the proceeds intended go to the general hospital. But hospital administrators refuse to take it, seeing the performers' desperate need for it as well.

Slowly the troupe disbands. Some find other work in town to pay their way home. Others walk south to Pembina, performing along the way to get home. Equipment—tents, wagons—remain in Winnipeg.

One of the clowns, Dick Burden, chooses to live in Winnipeg and becomes the first sign painter and bill poster.

1879

The first grain elevator on the Prairies is built in a community first known as Hespeler and now as Niverville.

The unique round structure is built by William

"We fed them hay and tended them in shelters much the same as domestic cattle," Alloway said.

The herds began to vanish again from Manitoba in 1879 "and from then on they were practically unknown," Alloway said.

On the vast prairies, the imprint left by the herds remained for decades—narrow trails from pastures to drinking places, "like lines of black ink crossing the grass which the sun yellowed to a parchment hue," William James Healy wrote in the 1927 book, *Winnipeg's Early Days*.

A trail that once crossed through the Winnipeg area could be seen long after the city was incorporated in 1873. It passed through what is now the Exchange District, not far from the Kay Building at the corner of McDermot Avenue and Arthur Street. That trail led to a place where the bison would drink and wallow in cool mud on the banks of the Red River, near the present site of the Provencher Bridge.

In interviews with the *Tribune* and *Winnipeg Free Press* in the 1920s, Alloway said the rate of the bison population's attrition coincided with the amplified pace of railway expansion threading across the prairies in the early 1870s.

Contractors for the rail companies hired hunters to supply the construction gangs with meat. Settlement then followed the rail lines and the land once grazed by the animals was desired by the new homesteaders. Hunts were organized, often for the sheer pleasure of the kill, with the animals being left to rot after their hides were stripped.

As firearms technology improved—double-barreled shotguns and repeating rifles replaced single-shot flintlocks—the efficiency of the kill quadrupled, and the bison were pushed further toward their end.

A June 1876 article in the *Free Press* advised people to store up on bison robes, predicting the extermination of the animal, between Lake of the Woods and the Rockies, within twelve to fourteen years.

MOUNTAINS OF BLEACHING BONES

The intensified large-scale slaughter led to the landscape being littered with bones bleaching under the summer sun. Settlers gathered them into towering mounds then shipped boxcar loads to the East where they were ground into powder to make fertilizer, chinaware, buttons, knife handles and in the sugar-refining process.

Bones at a railway siding in Saskatoon, Sask. Date unknown. GLENBOW LIBRARY AND ARCHIVES COLLECTION/UNIVERSITY OF CALGARY, CU196815

Before being named Regina (Latin for queen) in 1882, the Saskatchewan capital was known by a much less regal name. First Nations in the area called it oskana ka-asastēki, which roughly translates as bone piles. Europeans and settlers translated this to a handful of names along the same vein—Manybones, Bone Creek and primarily, Pile of Bones. It has been estimated the mounds near Wascana Creek measured six feet high and 40 feet in diameter at the base.

By 1884, it was estimated there were fewer than four hundred wild bison left. And by the end of that decade, they were essentially wiped off the continent.

In a 1912 report for the federal government, Winnipegger Isaac Cowie—who later compiled his memoirs in *The Company of Adventurers: A Narrative of Seven Years in the Service of the Hudson's Bay Company during 1867-1874*—wrote that the last known wild bison hunt happened in July 1888 when five were killed in the valley of the Red Deer River in Alberta.

ALLOWAY SELLS HERD

McKay died in December 1879 and Alloway reluctantly decided to join his brother's banking business.

The herd was sold to Col. Samuel Bedson, warden of Stony Mountain Penitentiary, for $1,000. He relocated it to land near the prison, close to what is now Oak Hammock Marsh. Bedson kept a collection of animals in a private zoo there, including bears, badgers, wolves, deer, moose, and game birds. Bedson's property also featured a curling rink, a horse track and the first golf course in Manitoba. The tee box for the Stony Mountain's first hole was immediately opposite Bedson's residence, and the course was a walk of about five kilometres from start to finish.

Samuel Bedson in 1873
PROVINCIAL ARCHIVES OF
MANITOBA, N10717

The nine-hole golf course was built by prisoners in 1889. It was among the earliest in all

Hespeler out of wood, and the first western Canadian barley ever shipped privately to overseas markets comes from that elevator.

January 23: The Historical and Scientific Society of Manitoba (now Manitoba Historical Society) is founded at a meeting inside the Main Street courthouse, making it the oldest organization in western Canada devoted to the promotion and preservation of historical resources.

It is officially incorporated by an act of the legislature on June 25, 1879.

1882

August 29: The first typewriter in the West is owned by Mr. Perkins, the official court stenographer.

The *Manitoba Free Press* calls it "a marvel of ingenuity," a machine "made so as to write either capital or lower-case letters at the will of the operator, who plays on the keyboard, something after the fashion of a person fingering a piano."

1883

February 9: The Winnipeg Rowing Club, first in the West, is formed with 150 members.

Six years later, Winnipeg's four-oar crew wins the international championship in Illinois.

March 19: The first cycling club is formed to establish the rights of "wheelmen" to be on the road, even though, at the time, a city bylaw prohibits the riding of bicycles within city limits.

A resolution from the club notes that "doctors and even clergymen ride wheels in other cities."

In time, the bylaw is lifted, and bicycle paths are created along Portage Avenue, on both sides of the streetcar tracks, from Main Street to Deer Lodge. On summer evenings, hundreds of cyclists—women as well as

Cyclist on Portage Avenue at Silver Heights, circa 1900
PROVINCIAL ARCHIVES OF MANITOBA, N4549

men—including some on tandem bicycles, make use of those paths, according to the book, *Winnipeg's Early Days*, published in 1927.

Some bicycle advertisements in the spring of 1883 showed young women "dashing in voluminous bloomers that indiscreetly revealed not only their ankles, but a few inches of their lower limbs," according to *Tales of Early Manitoba from the Winnipeg Free Press*, a book by Edith Paterson.

The city's forefathers didn't think that was appropriate for women, so in 1890, they passed the bicycle bylaw, which forbade the wearing of bloomers while cycling. It also prohibited the riding of bicycles or tricycles on sidewalks, while requiring riders to sound a gong or bell at a reasonable distance before passing any carriage, horse, cow, mule or other beast of burden or foot passenger.

September 18: A crematorium is used in the Northwest for the first time.

The carcasses of ten horses and two cows, along with remains from the slaughterhouse that had accumulated the week prior, are cremated.

North America. The first course was established in Montreal in 1873, and the first one in the United States opened in 1884 in West Virgina.

It's clear Manitobans were new to the sport, with the inaugural game resulting in double-digit scores on several holes, including 16, 17, 18 and 20. The game was played by two teams with partners taking turns hitting. The final tally for each team was 97 and 113.

"Taken all around, the Stony Mountain link is a hard one, knolls, bunkers, ploughed land, burnt prairie bushes, and long grass all helping its diversity. Although it was somewhat of a makeshift course, people came from far and near to enjoy the game of golf," the *Manitoba Free Press* reported in 1889.

While those attractions drew crowds to Stony Mountain, Bedson's bison were less eager to be there, at least initially. About 24 hours after being moved 20 kilometres north from their former residence on McKay's property, the animals escaped overnight and walked back to Deer Lodge through deep snow.

Bedson made the trip south the next morning to retrieve the animals. They were all marched back, including a day-old calf born almost immediately after the bison arrived at his property the first time.

"The vitality of the Individual buffalo has always been a matter of astonishment to me," Alloway told the *Tribune* in 1925. "No domestic calf could do one-quarter of that at the same age."

According to the Manitoba Historical Society, Alloway's widow, Maude, said her husband didn't fully abandon his bison preservation efforts after selling the herd. He went on a third, and final, excursion in 1883 and came back with "a number of fine specimen" from Alberta's Battle River area. They were kept at Deer Lodge until being bought years later by the Winnipeg's Street Railway Company for its zoo at River Park, at the south end of Osborne Street.

In the meantime, Bedson's bison multiplied to nearly 130. The warden loved to host parties and even trained some of his animals, such as moose, to pull a toboggan to provide rides to his guests.

He attempted the same thing with the bison, but it didn't pan out so well.

Bedson's daughter recalled her dad hitching a toboggan to a two-year-old bison one Christmas afternoon while eight guests settled onto the sled. Five inmates from the prison, brought over by Bedson to help with the party hospitalities, gripped a rope tied around the animal's broad neck.

The stoic bison simply stood there for fifteen to twenty minutes, then suddenly "took a terrible leap into the air. The rope broke and the prisoners and guests were scattered far and wide in the snow" as the bison galloped off and disappeared into the horizon. The story was told to Edith Paterson, who included it in her 1970 book, *Tales of Early Manitoba*.

The following spring, Bedson received a letter postmarked from North Dakota. A bison with a frayed rope around its neck was found wandering around the area. Bedson sent someone off to bring the animal back.

By 1888 an influx of settlement in the region prompted Bedson to part with his herd. Six

Charles Allard Jr.
LUXTON FAMILY FONDS/WHYTE MUSEUM OF THE CANADIAN ROCKIES

Michel Pablo
MALCOLM GEDDES FONDS/WHYTE MUSEUM OF THE CANADIAN ROCKIES

were donated to zoos in New York and London. Another twenty-seven were given to Donald Smith, a leading figure in the Hudson Bay Company's operations and in the creation of the CPR, to repay a loan he gave Bedson to originally buy the Alloway herd.

Smith, who famously drove the CPR's last spike in 1885, kept his animals for a few years on his Silver Heights estate, immediately west of Deer Lodge. The remaining animals went to Charles Jesse "Buffalo" Jones, manager of Garden City Buffalo Company in Kansas, who had spoken for years of wanting to create a game preserve for people to hunt bison for a fee. Some Winnipeggers tried unsuccessfully to prevent that by forming a company and trying to buy the bison to raise them commercially. Jones never created the game preserve, though.

Instead, the man who once boasted of having killed more buffalo than any other man, recognized the grim toll his pursuits had taken and, like Alloway, became determined to preserve them. His idea was to breed them with cattle to produce a stock hardy enough to survive the high plains, yet gentle enough to herd and brand. His so-called cattalo experiment failed because the species did not reproduce well.

A national recession in the early 1890s sent Jones into debt and he was forced to sell his bison. Most went to Charles Allard and Michel Pablo, ranchers in Montana who already had about a dozen of the animals.

Smith, meanwhile, was moving to Eastern Canada to take on the role as president of the Bank of Montreal, so he donated five of his bison to the City of Winnipeg, which was planning a new park and zoo. The animals remained on the Silver Heights estate until City Park opened in 1904, later to become Assiniboine Park and Zoo.

Smith's other twenty-two bison went to the Canadian government, which had started its own

Bison at Assiniboine Park Zoo in 1919, when it was still known as City Park
PROVINCIAL ARCHIVES OF MANITOBA, GEORGE HARRIS FONDS

conservation efforts—efforts that had a dark secondary motive: to assert control over Indigenous people by starving them into assimilating. The animals were shipped to Banff National Park to join a handful of wild ones first gathered in 1897.

The Allard-Pablo herd flourished in Montana and numbered three hundred by 1896 when

Alex Ayotte with bison calf. Date unknown.

LUXTON FAMILY FONDS/
WHYTE MUSEUM OF THE
CANADIAN ROCKIES

Allard died. His half was divided among his heirs, many of whom sold them to zoos and game farms.

Charles Allard Jr. and his brother Joseph merged their herds with Pablo's and a fourth man for a total of 250 animals, which grew to nearly 800 by 1906. But by then Montana's population was growing and the men were forced to disperse the animals to make room for settlement. They offered to sell them to the US government, but the authorities were only willing to pay $15 a head.

Canada offered $245 a head and two Manitobans played key roles in getting the Montana bison to Canada—Norman Luxton, son of *Manitoba Free Press* co-founder William F. Luxton, and Alexander Ayotte, a Canadian immigration agent stationed in Montana and originally from St. Jean-Baptiste, south of Winnipeg.

They joined with federal Minister of the Interior Frank Oliver and Banff National Park superintendent Howard Douglas to purchase 716

"...the greatest animal comeback in the history of the world"

Manitoba Historical Society

Norman Luxton
LUXTON FAMILY FONDS/
WHYTE MUSEUM OF THE
CANADIAN ROCKIES

bison. Luxton, then living in Banff, convinced Oliver, a close friend, that Canada should go after the Allard-Pablo herd. Oliver then convinced Ottawa, "setting the necessary wheels turning to advance what's often been heralded as the greatest animal comeback in the history of the world," according to the Manitoba Historical Society.

Ayotte negotiated the purchase and oversaw the roundups, which took nearly three years. Douglas arranged for the bison to go to zoos and parks, including his own and Manitoba's Riding Mountain National Park.

Wood Buffalo National Park, which spans the border between northeastern Alberta and the southern Northwest Territories—the second-largest national park in the world—was created specifically in 1922 as a bison range. The animals there have since become the world's largest free-roaming herd with an estimated 3,500.

There are now about 400,000 bison on the continent. In Canada alone, the 2016 census reported just under 120,000.

The small herd started by Alloway was the nucleus for it all.

WHEN KENORA WAS IN MANITOBA ... AND ONTARIO

Kenora in the 1880s was little more than a village set in a bush clearing in northeastern Manitoba. Or was it northwestern Ontario? For a while, either would have been correct. Or not. It was a confusing time. Like petulant children, each province laid claim to the territory known then as Rat Portage and refused to acknowledge the other's dubious authority. That led to a doubling of everything: laws, mayors and councils, constables, coroners, courts, and schools. Residents even had two political representatives—one for each provincial legislature. Because of that chaos, the small community in the wilds of western Canada became the focal point of a boundary dispute that went all the way to the Privy Council of England.

Main Street, Rat Portage in the 1880s THE MUSE LAKE
OF THE WOODS MUSEUM & DOUGLAS FAMILY ART CENTRE

Falls on Winnipeg River at Rat Portage, 1857 DIGITAL ARCHIVE ONTARIO/BALDWIN COLLECTION OF CANADIANA

Fall at Rat Portage

Beginning of Winnipeg River

Set on the north shore of Lake of the Woods, where the Winnipeg River begins its 235-kilometre course to Lake Winnipeg, Rat Portage was a key fur trade centre along the main canoe route to the West. The original Ojibwe name for the north end of Lake of the Woods was Wauzhushk Onigum, which translated to "portage to the country of the muskrat." It referred to the annual migration of muskrats between the lake and Winnipeg River. Rat Portage was the shortened version adopted by the Hudson's Bay Company for their trading post, which was established in 1836 on an island now known as Old Fort Island.

The post was moved in 1861 to the mainland and became the nucleus of the community that emerged around it. Located near the present-day corner of First Street South and Main Street South, the post grew into a small fort, consisting of three log houses roofed with bark and surrounded by a wood palisade. It was the first known European structure within today's boundaries of Kenora.

When Confederation took place in 1867, creating the provinces of New Brunswick, Nova Scotia, Quebec, and Ontario, the new Dominion of Canada reached from the Atlantic Ocean to the Great Lakes. West of that was the vast fur-trading territory known as Rupert's Land, granted to the Hudson's Bay Company in 1670 by the British Crown. It included all of what is now Manitoba, most of Saskatchewan, southern and central Alberta, southern Nunavut, northern Quebec, and northern Ontario. It also included a section of the northern US, encompassing parts of Minnesota, North and South Dakota, and Montana. Those areas were ceded to the US in the Treaty of 1818, paving the way for an international boundary. In November 1869, the HBC relinquished its rights over most of the territory. It surrendered its charter to the British Crown

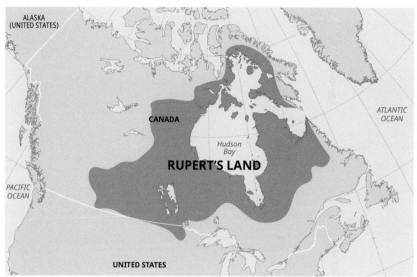

Map of 1817 showing Lord Selkirk's land grant of 116,000 square miles, known as Assiniboia. LIBRARY AND ARCHIVES CANADA

and received £300,000, or $1.5 million, in compensation. The transaction was authorized by the British Parliament, which then transferred the territory to the Dominion of Canada's authority. The HBC retained some trading posts and land for immigration and settlement. However,

Watercolour painting showing Hudson Bay Company post at Rat Portage in 1857 DIGITAL ARCHIVE ONTARIO/BALDWIN COLLECTION OF CANADIANA

Riel wanted to protect the freedom of the people in the Red River area as Canada looked to expand its Confederation footprint. His provisional government presented a list of rights that became the basis of the Manitoba Act. The province's original boundaries were squared off, creating an area just one-eighth of the present size (33,280 square kilometres compared to 649,950), which prompted the nickname "postage-stamp province." The northern border was near present-day Winnipeg Beach and the southern edge was the international border. To the west, it went just past Portage la Prairie and to the east it stopped around Elma, loosely marked by Highway 11—about 55 kilometres from the current Manitoba-Ontario border.

It wasn't long before Manitoba's political leaders pursued an expansion to the boundaries and sent a delegation to meet with the federal government in 1873. Its pitch? A breadth of 768,000 square kilometres, taking it north to Hudson Bay and east to Lake Superior, giving it two marine ports.

because of the political disruption of the Red River Resistance, the transfer did not come into effect until July 1870. That resistance, driven by Louis Riel, led the Red River colonists into Confederation and made Manitoba the fifth province in May 1870.

The proposed eastern boundary was similar to what, in 1811, had been granted by the HBC to Lord Selkirk,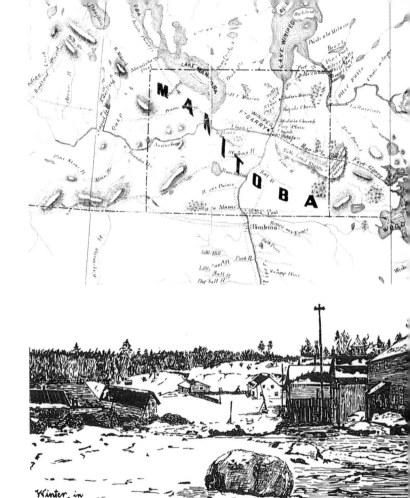

who brought in many of the Red River colonists to populate Manitoba around the Red and Assiniboine rivers. Selkirk's 300,400-square-kilometre territory, which he named Assiniboia, had stretched nearly to Fort William (Thunder Bay) on Lake Superior.

Prime Minister Sir John A. Macdonald was receptive to Manitoba's request but was forced to resign in November 1873 due to the Pacific Scandal—allegations of large sums of money paid by private interests to his government to influence bidding on the Canadian Pacific Railway construction project. His party then lost the election in early 1874 and Manitoba's expansion was shelved.

The exact range of Ontario's western edge had become a political issue as well. The original 1867 description put the boundary at the point where it met Rupert's Land. But with Rupert's Land

Winter in Rat Portage, 1875 *HISTORICAL REVIEW OF RAT PORTAGE AND LAKE OF THE WOODS TO COMMEMORATE JUBILEE JAMBOREE CELEBRATION, JUNE 28TH TO JULY 1ST 1952*

Firsts in the Northwest 1889-1898

1889

September 3: The cornerstone of the first Hebrew synagogue in the Northwest is laid.

Shaarey Zedek, which means the Gates of Righteousness, is built on the corner of King and Common (now Henry) streets in Winnipeg.

1891

January 17: Winnipeg's first electric streetcar makes its maiden run, establishing that service in the city before Toronto, Montreal and even New York City.

Postcard shows the Park Line streetcar approaching Edison Hall in River Park. The tracks would be along what is now South Osborne Street. No date is given but the postcard's mailing year is 1907.
WINNIPEG PUBLIC LIBRARY

no longer in existence it was unclear where this boundary should be.

In 1876, Prime Minister Sir Alexander Mackenzie created the District of Keewatin to better administer Canada's western territories. It encompassed the bulk of what is now Manitoba, Northwestern Ontario and southern Nunavut. The act that established the district declared the governor of Manitoba to be ex-officio lieutenant governor for Keewatin to "make provision for the administration of justice ... and establish all such laws."

A Council of Keewatin was formed with members mainly from Manitoba. Unsurprisingly, the laws put in place were similar to those in Manitoba.

An 1874 Royal Commission recommended the Manitoba-Ontario borderline be set through the Northwest Angle of Lake of the Woods—the location it is today—but a board of arbiters didn't endorse the recommendation until 1878. By then, Macdonald had returned to power and ignored the arbiters' decision.

With Macdonald back in the Prime Minister's chair, Manitoba sent another delegation to meet with the federal government on the issue of expansion, citing more urgency as the province's population was rapidly growing and putting strain on its borders. As well, thousands more people had begun homesteading beyond Manitoba's borders and had no political representation. The province was also concerned about control over natural resources and public lands in the region, neither of which were being appropriately managed as they fell outside of Manitoba's authority.

As a result, in 1881, Manitoba's borders were

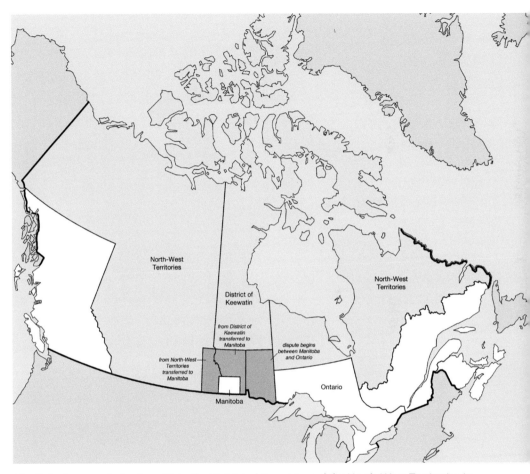

Manitoba is expanded outward into the District of Keewatin and the North-West Territories in 1881, beginning the dispute with Ontario. WIKIMEDIA CREATIVE COMMONS, USER: GOLBEZ

1892

Manitoba becomes first province to hold a referendum on Prohibition in Canada. Although Manitobans vote in favour, the legislation is never put into effect. In 1899, another referendum is held, and another majority of voters support the ban, but the vote is later nullified because of low turnout.

Prohibition does come to Manitoba in March 1916 after a third referendum on the topic. The Manitoba Temperance Act comes into effect. All legal drinking establishments are closed.

Bootlegging flourishes and Manitobans skirt the law through illegal pubs known as speakeasies. Doctor prescriptions for alcohol, which are supposed to be strictly for medicinal purposes, are widely abused and hardly hidden as long line-ups become common at pharmacies.

In 1921, just five years after prohibition was declared, it ends. Manitobans vote to allow the sale of alcohol through a provincial government agency.

1893

October 2: The first electric elevator in the Northwest takes on its first passenger.

Ryan's boot and shoe store
SEVEN OAKS HOUSE MUSEUM/
SEVENOAKSHOUSE.CA

It was added inside a four-storey building at 492 Main St., between Bannatyne and William avenues in Winnipeg in 1893. The building was constructed in 1883 for shoe merchant Thomas Ryan. His business was the largest of its kind in Canada, with customers between Lake Superior and British Columbia.

A person of strong faith, Ryan had an inscription carved in stone and set at the top of the store: "The Earth is the Lord's and the Fullness Thereof." When the cornerstone was laid May 21, 1883, he allegedly placed into the cavity a leather bag containing dust from the valley of the River Jordan, a stone from Solomon's Temple and some leaves from the banks of the Pool of Solomon.

A fire in 1933 reduced the building (which had

expanded to five times their original size, to 189,327 square kilometres. But its eastern border line remained amorphous, simply described as the "western border of Ontario," which was still undefined and in dispute. Meanwhile, things were picking up around Rat Portage, where the HBC was selling parcels of its land to eager settlers. Houses sprang up near the post. General stores, hotels, saloons, flour and lumber mills were established, and work crews flooded in to build the railway. Timber in the area was a valuable construction material and gold had been discovered. It all caused debate over who owned the land as well as the resource and mineral rights and royalties.

Manitoba provincial jail in Rat Portage, 1883 THE MUSE LAKE OF THE WOODS MUSEUM & DOUGLAS FAMILY ART CENTRE

Manitoba moved to assert authority, taking its cue from the laws set up by the Keewatin Act. It established a judicial system, appointed a coroner and issuer of marriage licences, set out the electoral district and enacted its own legislation on liquor.

On July 22, 1882, as a result of a petition to Manitoba, the town of Rat Portage was

been sold in 1900 to a home furnishings company) to two storeys and destroyed the façade. It is not known if the items Ryan originally placed in the cornerstone still exist.

November 13: A steam cider, the first in the Northwest, is installed in the Blackwood's Beverages plant in Winnipeg. The first fresh cider was bottled the following month using apples imported from Ontario.

1898

September 15: Two Russian families arrive in Winnipeg to scout it as a possible new home for a persecuted sect from Russia.

Four months later, on January 27, 1899, the first party of Doukhobors begin their new lives. Before the end of that year, there are 7,427.

Rat Portage mill, 1897 DIGITAL ARCHIVE ONTARIO/BALDWIN COLLECTION OF CANADIANA

incorporated under the laws of that province. Only a month earlier, on June 11, the first-ever train into Rat Portage arrived from Winnipeg. The ties to Manitoba were being well established.

Not to be outdone, Ontario incorporated Rat Portage as a township under its provincial laws on August 22, 1883. It set up similar structures of government and both provinces proceeded to issue titles to mining claims and lumber licences.

Prisoners sent to jail by one province were released by the other, and constables who made arrests were themselves arrested by constables of the other province, according to the Manitoba Historical Society. At one point, the Manitoba jail was stormed and burned. Premier John Norquay, along with a force of police, travelled by special train from Winnipeg to arrest those responsible.

In September 1883, polling took place to elect members to the legislatures of both provinces. Manitoba employed a militia force in Rat Portage to protect its polls.

"Rat Portage had the most, but undoubtedly the worst, government ever known in Canada," wrote Douglas Kemp in the Manitoba Historical Society's magazine, *Manitoba Pageant*, in April 1956.

While officers arrested one another—and even judges—on trumped-up charges, the gamblers and whisky pedlars enjoyed almost complete immunity, wrote Det.-Sgt. John Burchill in *The Rat Portage War*. "It was next to impossible for a constable, zealous as he might be in

Prisoners sent to jail by one province were released by the other, and constables who made arrests were themselves arrested by constables of the other province.

Woodley & Lang's shipyard in Rat Portage, 1897

Rat Portage mill, 1897 DIGITAL ARCHIVE ONTARIO/
BALDWIN COLLECTION OF CANADIANA

Steamer at Kendall's Wharf in Rat Portage, 1897 DIGITAL ARCHIVE ONTARIO/BALDWIN COLLECTION OF CANADIANA

the discharge of his duty, to observe the actions of evil-doers, while he himself was a fugitive from justice, engaged in dodging a warrant for his own arrest."

The absurdity came to a head in November 1883 when Ontario's chief of police arrested Manitoba's chief of police during a squabble over a shopkeeper being charged by Manitoba police for selling liquor without a licence.

The shopkeeper claimed he had an Ontario permit but was ordered to appear before a Manitoba judge. The Ontario police advised him to ignore the summons and stationed a squad of officers to prevent his arrest. When Manitoba constables showed up for the arrest, both forces began assaulting and handcuffing one another.

That led to the appointment of a single commissioner of police for the territory and the merger of both town councils into a single municipal board until the dispute was resolved. The attorneys-general of both

In 1905 Rat Portage became Kenora, a name derived from the first two letters from each of the sister communities of Keewatin, Norman, and Rat Portage.

Rat Portage, 1897 DIGITAL ARCHIVE ONTARIO/
BALDWIN COLLECTION OF CANADIANA

provinces agreed to allow the Queen's Privy Council (the highest law in Canada at the time) to settle the matter once and for all.

Geographically, it makes more sense for Kenora to be part of Manitoba. It's 180 kilometres directly east of Winnipeg yet 410 kilometres from Thunder Bay, which is the closest major Ontario centre. It's more than 1,320 kilometres from Ontario's provincial capital, Toronto. In fact, it's closer to the capitals of both Saskatchewan and Alberta than it is to Toronto.

Nonetheless, on August 11, 1884, the disputed territory was granted to Ontario, upholding the 1878 arbiters' decision.

In 1905 Rat Portage became Kenora, a name derived from the first two letters from each of the sister communities of **Ke**ewatin, **No**rman, and **Ra**t Portage.

BERGEN CUTOFF
THE PATH OF UNFULFILLED PROMISE

A six-kilometre straightaway cuts through north Winnipeg like a faded scar. It's a little wider than the 4-foot-8-inch gap between the set of railroad tracks that once ran along it. As a rail line, the path was a valuable grain link that ran into the heart of what was planned to be a grand railyard at the heart of a new city called North Transcona. It is now mostly forgotten, overgrown and rewilded in some places, squeezed out by new housing developments in others. The promised city never transpired, and most of the buildings—a hotel, school, and post office among them—have long since collapsed or been demolished.

The most visible remnant of the Canadian Pacific Railway's Bergen Cutoff line is an abandoned truss bridge many Winnipeggers have seen but might not know much about. The iron span across the Red River, between North and West Kildonan, has been abandoned for nearly a hundred years. The middle of its three sections is swung open as if waiting for passing steamboats that haven't plied the river for just as long.

Aerial view of the Canadian Pacific Railway Bergen Cutoff Bridge with Kildonan Settlers Bridge in the background, June 2017 GORDON GOLDSBOROUGH

A golfer tees off at hole #10 of the Kildonan Park Golf Course with the Bergen overpass cutting through.
DARREN BERNHARDT

North Transcona CPR station TRANSCONA MUSEUM AND ARCHIVES/ WINNIPEG RAILWAY MUSEUM FONDS TH98.92.1

Other vestiges of the Bergen line are two grassy hills on either side of Main Street, between the North End sewage treatment centre and Kildonan Golf Course. They're part of the old railbed, raised at that location to pass above the Main Street traffic. The overpass platform was long ago removed, but the embankment still runs through the golf course, making for a unique experience on the tenth hole. It ends at the riverbank where it meets the truss bridge.

A similar set of embankments also existed on either side of Henderson Highway, near Springfield Road, but were carved down as the area's residential development was expanded.

The Bergen name came from a small station stop northwest of Winnipeg, off Rosser Road within the city's current Perimeter Highway loop. The station, which had a single grain elevator, was part of the CPR's Carberry subdivision and the western terminus of the Bergen line. The eastern terminus was a point called Norcan (North Transcona) on the CPR's Keewatin subdivision.

In all, the line took up 518 hectares of land and was an alternate route—a cutoff—to the CPR's newly built north yards. The yards were created in 1912 to alleviate pressure on the company's main yards at Arlington Street and Dufferin in central Winnipeg.

At the time, the CPR was experiencing surging demand to move grain and other imports between the Atlantic and Pacific Coasts. European and Asian shippers found it easiest to send goods in a ship across the ocean to a Canadian port, then load them onto rail cars and haul them to the other coast. There, the goods would be reloaded onto another ship for the next ocean passage. Canada was essentially used as a shortcut.

The CPR's central yards in Winnipeg were already congested and becoming enveloped by a rapidly growing city that limited the company's ability to expand its footprint. In addition to the booming construction of housing and industry, the city was being stitched by

The CPR devised an ambitious plan to bypass Winnipeg through the farmland well north—at that time—of the city's limits.

A CP passenger train passes through Bergen station stop, August 1936. UNIVERSITY OF WINNIPEG ARCHIVES, WESTERN CANADA PICTORIAL INDEX/GURLING COLLECTION, A0761-22912

Firsts in the Northwest 1902-1913

1902

May 27: Manitoba Society of Artists is established in the studio of Frank Milton Armington in Winnipeg's Hargrave Block.

The society's purpose is to promote and encourage visual artists in the province as a western equivalent to the Ontario Society of Artists.

Notable past members include Lionel LeMoine FitzGerald (the only member of the Group of Seven based in western Canada, Eric Bergman, Leo Mol, Alex J. Musgrove, Clarence Tellenius, Walter J. Phillips, Lynn Sissons, Kelly Clark, Caroline Dukes, Tony Tascona, and Robert Bruce.

1904

March 12: Winnipeg Automobile Club is formed at the home of Edgar Boteler Kenrick, 282 Assiniboine Ave.

Kenrick was the first person in Winnipeg to own a car, in 1901. Seven years later there were three hundred automobiles registered in the city.

November: Canada's tallest building, the eleven-storey Union Bank Building, officially opens

tracks from four railroad companies serving it. So, the CPR devised an ambitious plan to bypass Winnipeg through the farmland well north—at that time—of the city's limits. New switching yards were to be located north of Transcona, a town that was also built by the railroad industry when the Grand Trunk Pacific and National Transcontinental Railway arrived.

Transcona's name is derived from **Trans**continental and Strath**cona**, the latter being Lord Strathcona, aka Donald Smith, a former Manitoba politician instrumental in building the CPR and the person who drove its last spike in British Columbia.

The vision for North Transcona was a city of 50,000 residents and thousands more employees working the vast railyard between Springfield and Cordite roads, off Lagimodiere Boulevard. Planning began in 1911 and construction for the yards was well underway in 1912, the same year Transcona was incorporated as a town. In March 1912, the CPR purchased the land it required for the Bergen route, paying $385,000 (equivalent to nearly $12 million today).

BIG PLANS

North Transcona was to be centred just west of what was then called King Street (now Plessis Road), close to Grassie Boulevard. William Grassie was a real estate agent involved in the development. This area was considered ideally connected to Winnipeg via Grassie, and to Birds Hill, the community just north of the city.

A land survey was completed, outlining a plan for residential areas with graded streets, some 22 kilometres of sidewalks, a railway station and local businesses including a hotel, post office,

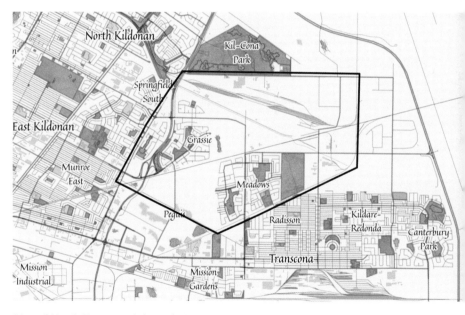

A 1912 advertisement for the North Transcona townsite in *The Voice*, weekly newspaper by the Winnipeg Trades and Labour Council
COMMUNITIES THAT TIME FORGOT, MARCH 7, 2023/ TRANSCONAMUSEUM.MB.CA

Map of North Transcona's boundaries COMMUNITIES THAT TIME FORGOT, MARCH 7, 2023/TRANSCONAMUSEUM.MB.CA

at the corner of William Avenue and Main Street in Winnipeg. It is also the second-tallest building in the entire British Empire.

The Union Bank tower, as it became known, continues to be the oldest existing example in Canada of skyscraper construction using a steel skeleton structure—a design innovation that facilitated the proliferation of towers in the twentieth century.

The term skyscraper now, however, is reserved for buildings greater than forty storeys.

1907

September: The Western Associated Press, forerunner to the Canadian Press, is created by the heads of three Winnipeg newspapers.

Robert Lorne Richardson (publisher of the *Tribune*) and Mark Edgar Nichols (president and editor of the *Telegram*) gather with the *Manitoba Free Press'* general manager Edward Hamilton Macklin and editor-in-chief John Wesley Dafoe after their papers are all sent a note from the Canadian Pacific Railway Telegraph Company.

The CPR, through its telegraph, held a monopoly

banks, and several commercial and retail venues. Newspaper advertisements and brochures started hailing North Transcona as "the future railroad, factory and labour centre of Winnipeg."

The townsite's approximate borders were—based on present-day arteries—Molson Street (west), Springfield Road (north), midway between Day and Redonda streets (east), and a southern boundary line that is closely followed by the current rail line and then along Transcona Boulevard-Ravelston Avenue West-Callsbeck Avenue back to Molson. Acreages were offered up for $300, while average lots 30 feet wide by 100 feet deep ranged between $12 to $32 per foot.

Manufacturing companies such as Manitoba Bridge and Iron Works, Dominion Tar and Chemical Co., the Hughes Manufacturing Co., and the Eley Cartridge Co. signed on to open plants in the industrial area adjacent to the railyards.

The post office opened in 1913 along present-day Bluecher Avenue. Close by was the railway station, at the current intersection of Day Street and

Risque Avenue. The land occupied by the station is now a self-storage business.

A thirty-six-room, three-storey hotel was built at King Street and Van Horne Avenue just south of the yards and the one-room North Transcona School (later Beaman School), opened in 1914 on the north side of Springfield—land that is now part of Kilcona Park.

The railyards were constructed with both east-bound and westbound receiving and departure sections, a modern feature for the time that could handle large numbers of boxcars every day. Both sections had forty tracks and each track could hold seventy-two cars. There were machine shops, a powerhouse, office buildings, repair and transfer facilities, caboose storage and locomotive yard, coal storage track and dock, thirty-stall roundhouse, water tower, 170 kilometres of track and 366 switches. The site had a capacity for some 12,000 railcars with a turntable able to handle 30-metre-long locomotives. Completed at a cost of $4 million, the yards were fully functional by May 1914.

SINKING FEELING

One of the earliest structures foreshadowed the fate of North Transcona. A massive grain elevator of reinforced concrete, featuring an annex with sixty-five silos standing side-by-side like soldiers, was built in 1912 and designed to store as much as one million bushels of grain brought in from rural elevators across the prairies.

The annex began sinking and listing in October 1913 after being filled. The clay-and-soil gumbo that makes up much of the Red River Valley couldn't withstand the weight.

When it finally stabilized itself, twelve hours after it began tilting, it was at a 30-degree

The tilted CPR North Transcona Parrish & Heimbecker grain elevator in October 1913.
PROVINCIAL ARCHIVES OF MANITOBA/L.B. FOOTE COLLECTION, N2793

angle. Holes were then bored into the silos to empty the grain.

A new foundation, this time reaching to the bedrock, was constructed underneath the lopsided structure. The annex was then straightened again and exists to this day, though it has not been used since late 2021.

The incident has become a case study for the geotechnical industry.

BERGEN BRIDGE

In the meantime, construction on the Bergen line was underway with work on the truss bridge starting in 1913. A base camp was set up on the river's east bank to house work crews. Bunkhouses, a dining room, and a cook house were erected along with separate residences for the project's superintendent and foremen.

The Red River was a navigable waterway at the time—allowing river traffic from the US through to Lake Winnipeg and beyond—so the new bridge required a swing section to allow vessels to pass. The bridge was 284 metres long and almost 10 metres wide to accommodate two sets of tracks. It had seven large piers sunk six metres into bedrock, making it strong enough to support two trains simultaneously.

The *Keenora* steamer passes the Bergen Cutoff bridge in 1939. PROVINCIAL ARCHIVES OF MANITOBA/GEORGE HARRIS FONDS

The first train crossing happened May 1, 1914. But just three months later the Panama Canal opened, and the CPR's fortunes abruptly changed.

The first train crossing happened on May 1, 1914. But just three months later the Panama Canal opened, and the CPR's fortunes abruptly changed.

Carved through the isthmus between North and South America, the canal created an all-water shipping route. Despite being some 4,800 kilometres south of Winnipeg, it had a direct impact on the city. The CPR experienced a sudden and substantial downturn in traffic from foreign markets which favoured using the Panama Canal rather than the train route across Canada.

since 1894 in the distribution of the Associated Press wire service in Canada.

The note says it is cutting back the daily wire feed while boosting the fee. Under the old plan, the AP report from the east contained international news and a summary of Canadian news. With the new plan, the AP report would come from St. Paul, Minnesota at twice the cost and Canadian content would be available separately for another fee.

The newspaper publishers are infuriated enough to look past their rivalries and political oppositions to form a united front. They sign up with three non-AP services—United Press, Publishers' Press, and Laffan's—and establish special correspondents to contribute to the pool.

The group then applies for, and is granted, a charter for Western Associated Press by the Manitoba government.

The WAP signs up other western papers then expands east as its popularity grows. The CPR, at one point, tries to raise wire rates for the newspapers but publishers and owners rally to fight the new rates and the railway relents.

Weary of the fighting and the bad publicity, the

CPR turns over the AP rights to WAP and the eastern papers. In January 1911, the WAP became The Canadian Press Limited.

1908

January 15: The Manitoba government acquires Bell Telephones' operations and equipment in the province and the first publicly owned telephone system on the continent goes into operation.

April 12: The first air-filling station in Winnipeg for the tires of cars and cyclists is set up by the *Manitoba Free Press* at the curb on Garry Street. The newspaper's offices were located at that time at the corner of Portage Avenue and Garry. The line was connected to the plant's air compressor.

July: Winnipeg's first playground opens on the shared grounds of Albert and Victoria schools, bounded by Bannatyne and William avenues, and Gertie and Ellen streets.

1912

March 12: The Industrial Bureau Exposition Building opens to the public at the corner of Main Street and Water Avenue (now William Stephenson Way) in Winnipeg.

It showcases products and innovations by

Industrial Bureau Exposition Building, 1912   INTERNET ARCHIVE/PUBLIC DOMAIN

government, businesses, industries, and individuals. It also has a convention hall, public market and a civic art gallery and museum. The latter, which opens in December, is the first admission-free venue of its kind in North America.

July: Winnipeg's John Armstrong "Army" Howard is chosen during a time of overt racism to represent Canada in four events at the 1912 summer Olympic Games in Stockholm, Sweden: 100- and 200-metre sprints, 4x100m relay team and 4x400m relay team. With that, he

The onset of the First World War also had its effect. Expansion plans for the North Transcona yards—adding tracks, bunkhouses, a brickyard office building, and an icehouse—were immediately scrapped.

All of those changes, along with the world economic crash a decade after the war, meant rail traffic through the Winnipeg area never achieved the growth anticipated prior to 1914. Consequently, the city of North Transcona failed to develop. No more than two hundred people ever lived there. The hotel closed in 1918 and the yards never came close to the expected five thousand workers.

Many proposed streets are shown on early maps created in anticipation of North Transcona's emergence, but the vast majority were never built. And those that did exist were never anything but mud roads, according to Jim Smith, president, archivist, and historian with the North East Winnipeg Historical Society.

In December 1928, the CPR closed the North Transcona yards, firing 328 employees and relocating the remaining 800 to its central yard. The Bergen line was shut down at the same time. The post office lingered a bit longer until it closed in May 1932. The school remained in operation, serving the small population until it closed in 1952.

Today, dozens of tracks remain in the railyards, but the property only exists to store freight cars. The only rail access to the site is at the eastern flank. The line at the west edge was severed in 2011 by the new Chief Peguis Trail, cleaving the connection to the Bergen line.

Rail traffic through the Winnipeg area never achieved the growth anticipated prior to 1914.

The majority of the site's large structures were removed not long after it was shut down, but the roundhouse's chimney, which stood like a tall

breaks the colour barrier as the first Black athlete to be part of a Canadian Olympic team.

He isn't able to medal, though. And it won't be until 1934 that a Black Canadian athlete wins an Olympic medal. Hamilton's Ray Lewis will win bronze that year with the 4x400m men's relay team.

1913

Winnipeg becomes first city in North America, and third in the world, to install call boxes on street

Officers Joe Gallagher and Paul Otto wear buffalo coats and check in at Call Box 113, at the corner of Main Street and Alexander Avenue, in 1966. WINNIPEG POLICE MUSEUM & HISTORICAL SOCIETY

tombstone, remained until it was finally demolished in 2016. Somewhat appropriately, the yards now exist in the shadow of a scrapyard.

The area around the North Transcona yards may not resemble the once-grand plan, but it is far from abandoned. Many industries exist on both sides of the yards, some on the original dirt streets. As well, residential developments like Harbour View South and the Meadows are relatively newer subdivisions but were originally proposed way back in the original North Transcona city plans.

TRACK PRINTS

Most of the Bergen tracks were removed sometime in the 1950s but their ghost trail can still be seen in several places. It runs west from the yards, parallel to Springfield Road before tapering off at Gateway Road. Houses cover the path from there until Henderson Highway, where a 643-metre-long section leads to the riverbank and the truss bridge.

On the other side of the river, beyond the embankment in the golf course, tracks still exist

Most of the Bergen tracks were removed sometime in the 1950s but their ghost trail can still be seen in several places.

Looking north on Henderson Highway at the overpass for the Bergen Cutoff bridge in 1931. The building in background at left is Lord Kitchener School, now known as John Pritchard School. Just beyond the overpass is where Springfield Road is today. PROVINCIAL ARCHIVES OF MANITOBA

west of Main. They run between the water pollution control centre and Vince Leah Park before linking up with CPR's Selkirk line. The ghost path then re-emerges for about three kilometres from Ferrier Street before being obliterated by the Amber Trails neighbourhood at Pipeline Road.

Along the northern edge of that path are manufacturing companies, overgrown dormant farmland and a cemetery. To the south are new housing developments and mapped-out future developments. Some of the ghost path is being used as a gravel access road, one chunk is buried under a car dealership, and other stretches appear to have been mostly untouched since the rails were removed. They show up as long parallel strips of mud with grass growing in the middle.

BOOTLEGGING AND BOMBS

Prior to the tracks being removed, the abandoned line was still used on occasion—but not always for legitimate reasons. During the 1920s, it served as a bootlegging route to supply alcohol to the US during Prohibition. With the help of railmen who had access to a couple of boxcars and an engine, alcohol was loaded up and shipped in 45-gallon drums. Somewhere along the line, the cars were switched over to the Soo Line that ran to Chicago. During the Second World War, the truss bridge was used in mock scenarios to train soldiers on how to wire and blow-up bridges.

Over the years the bridge has been the subject of many proposed uses.

When the CPR removed the tracks, it also took out the bridge's timber decking and permanently opened the swing span. That's how it has been ever since. The cabin for the bridge operator, set along the bridge's top beam, remains. But there is no trace of any equipment, according to the Manitoba Historical Society.

Over the years the bridge has been the subject of many proposed uses. Provincial and municipal governments pursued it and much of the old Bergen path in the 1950s with the intention of creating a perimeter highway around Winnipeg. It was hoped that would also alleviate traffic issues in the northeast and take some pressure off the Redwood and Louise bridges.

City engineer William Donald Hurst, in 1953, said the Bergen bridge could be converted to highway use but would need to be widened and re-decked. The CPR refused to sell it, though, and the plans fizzled. Instead, the perimeter roadway and bridge were built three kilometres further north. The Disraeli Bridge also opened, in 1959, to ease the traffic congestion.

The city twice revisited the idea of incorporating the Bergen span into traffic plans—in 1962 and 1964. The idea was for an inner ring road but again the CPR wouldn't budge, even after a delegation went to Montreal to meet the CPR president.

Six decades later, the city is still working on that inner beltway. The Kildonan Settlers Bridge,

A speedboat passes the Bergen Cutoff bridge in July 2024.
DARREN BERNHARDT

just north of the truss bridge, opened in 1990, along with the first section of Chief Peguis Trail that links Lagimodiere Boulevard and Main Street. The city's intention is to eventually expand the trail to Route 90, which will at long last complete that inner loop.

As the Chief Peguis construction was underway, the CPR finally softened its grip on the truss

corners for police officers walking the beat.

The heavy cast-iron boxes, also called police signal boxes, are perched atop posts and large bases. Opened with a key, they contain a handset with a direct line to the local precinct. Officers are required to check in regularly, providing reports or getting instructions.

The boxes can also be used to request an ambulance or fire crew to an emergency, or to call for the police wagon to transport someone arrested by an officer who is on foot patrol. A dial is turned to a marker inside the box, then a crank is turned to send the signal.

The box is the most advanced communication system of any police agency on the continent but its use declines after the introduction of portable two-way radios in the 1960s.

bridge. It sold it in 1985, along with 8.9 hectares of the Bergen cutoff, to a group of three men with big dreams. In 1987, the new owners pitched a plan to convert the bridge into a restaurant and pedestrian corridor and build a forty-unit housing development on the east bank between the river and Henderson. The idea included a riverbank park, boat docks, skating rink, and cross-country ski trails in winter, and an ornamental hanging garden.

Conceptual drawing for the re-use of the Bergen Cutoff bridge.
THE BERGEN BRIDGE FACEBOOK PAGE/FACEBOOK.COM/BERGENBRIDGE

"We think we can create one of the most exciting places to go in Winnipeg," one the trio, Garry Hilderman, told the *Winnipeg Free Press*.

Much of the plan was withdrawn less than a year later when a community group opposed it. Primarily, they objected to development that would take away their green space and increase traffic in the area. In the three decades since the tracks had been removed, area residents were using the nearly six hectares of former CPR right-of-way between Henderson Highway and the river as a park. So in 1998, the city purchased that section for $400,000 and has retained it as a walking and cycling trail. It's called Bergen Cutoff Park.

The developers refocused their efforts, shifting the restaurant plan to the bridge's west spans, where visitors could have easier access through Kildonan Park. The men also owned the Bergen embankment that ran through the golf course.

Plans evolved many times over the next few years. One idea called for a high-end restaurant, family eatery, and banquet facility on the west span with the swing section and eastern span landscaped as a park. By 1994, the plans grew to include a golf element, to tie into the neighbouring course, where the developers hoped to arrange parking. The idea was for a pedestrian promenade along the bridge, with a combined golf club-house and fine-dining restaurant under the bridge, suspended above the river. The plan also involved a new eighteenth hole built on a barge, and a driving range that featured floating balls and a boom that would keep them from vanishing with the current. Each new idea was met either by resistance from residents or apathy on the part of city council to approve it.

By 2007, the plan was for restaurants below the west span and a garden above, with pumps feeding a large waterfall. Audio and visual displays were to be projected onto the waterfall, like a screen, to tell the history of the river—using its own water.

One of Hilderman's partners had sold his share in the project by that time, but Hilderman

The Bergen Cutoff bridge seen from the western end, in Kildonan Park, without the timber decking DARREN BERNHARDT

told the *Free Press* he hadn't given up on the idea because it "stretches the imagination."

But Hilderman died in 2016 without seeing anything happen with the bridge.

The iron span and small sections of riverbank on either side remain in private hands today, but nothing has changed—other than the size of trees growing where the tracks once met the bridge.

FUGITIVE TO FOLK HERO
SHOOTOUTS, HIDEOUTS, AND MANHUNTS FOR PERCY MOGGEY

He wasn't particularly intimidating—short and lean with a receding hairline that gave him a grandfatherly appearance. But the mythos created by Charles Percy Moggey, a brash gunslinging man who swung between charm and violence, was enormous. He's been called Manitoba's Jesse James, the Lone Wolf, and Manitoba's Bogeyman.

From 1923, when he first went to jail for selling home brew at the age of 19, the longest Moggey ever spent outside prison walls—as a legitimately free adult—was just four years: 1953-1957. His escapades ran the gamut of a police checklist: multiple jailbreaks and attempted jailbreaks, gunfights with police, auto theft, break-and-enter, robbery, trespassing, assault, possession of weapons that included handguns, rifles, knives, and explosives.

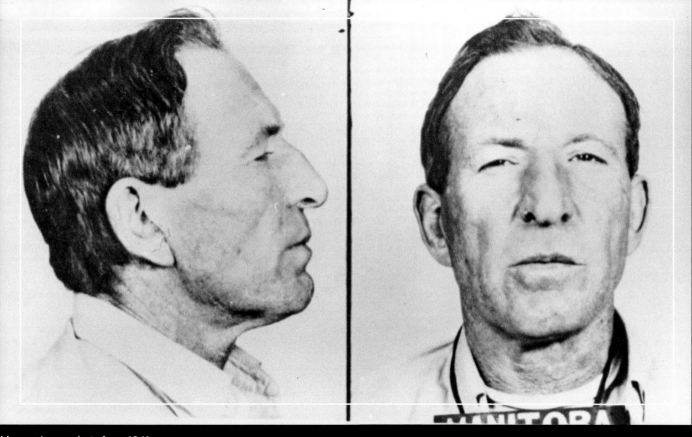

Moggey's mugshots from 1961 UNIVERSITY OF WINNIPEG ARCHIVES,
WESTERN CANADA PICTORIAL INDEX/*WINNIPEG TRIBUNE* COLLECTION, A0860-25699

Moggey was a Houdini-like master of lockpicking and escapes. He was 56 on July 25, 1960, when he somehow pried open the door and snuck out of his cell at Stony Mountain federal penitentiary around 11:30 p.m. He then scaled an eighteen-foot wall using a pole with a crudely attached meat hook wrapped in electrical tape.

Stony Mountain penitentiary as seen in 1966 PROVINCIAL ARCHIVES OF MANITOBA/ARCHITECTURAL SURVEY COLLECTIONS N20820

His absence wasn't discovered until 3:30 a.m. when a guard realized the mound in Moggey's bed was a makeshift dummy. That was two years before the same modus operandi was employed by three convicts to escape Alcatraz Island in California.

The pole and hook were later found hanging outside, the hook still attached to the handrail at the top of the wall.

At the time, Moggey was serving a ten-year sentence for break-and-enter, safecracking, trespassing and carrying a weapon, after an incident in Port Arthur (which became part of Thunder Bay in 1970). He had been convicted in November 1957.

Some newspaper reports say he was the first person to ever escape the prison north of Winnipeg but that's untrue. The first person did so in 1923 and

After sneaking from his cell, Moggey had to avoid guards and get through four locked doors. He never explained how he did it.

then another three men got away in 1938. Moggey did, however, manage to stay on the lam longer than anyone else.

After sneaking from his cell, Moggey had to avoid guards and get through four locked doors. He never explained how he did it, but news reports from the time said he was an experienced locksmith. He then passed through the prison kitchen and stocked up with as much food as he could carry, before heading to the exterior yard and going over the wall.

Stony Mountain from the inside. Date unknown. PROVINCIAL ARCHIVES OF MANITOBA, GR3552

Firsts in the Northwest 1916-1925

1916

January 28: Manitoba becomes the first province in Canada to grant women the right to vote—and to put themselves forward as candidates—in provincial elections. The law applies to all women except those who are First Nations, as they are subject to federal, not provincial law. Saskatchewan and Alberta follow Manitoba's lead in March and April, respectively, of 1916.

Canada grants women the right to vote federally in 1918. Quebec women finally win the right to vote in provincial elections in 1940 but not until 1960 are First Nations—women and men—allowed to vote in Canada without giving up treaty rights.

1917

April: The first Black labour union in North America is organized in Winnipeg by railway sleeping car porters who want to improve their working conditions. Other unions, such as the Canadian Brotherhood of Railroad Employees (CBRE), do not allow Black people as members, so the porters form their own: the Order of Sleeping Car Porters.

Black sleeping car porters PROVINCIAL ARCHIVES OF ALBERTA, A9167

One of the locations at which they meet regularly is a small assembly hall on the second floor of the Craig Block, next to the Sutherland Hotel on Main Street. The building remains to this day but has no markers indicating its significance.

December 6: Irvine Robbins, of Baskin-Robbins ice cream fame, is born in Winnipeg.

His family moves to Washington State while he is a young boy and Robbins's dad opens an ice-cream shop in Tacoma. After serving in the Second

The escape set off a massive manhunt and captured the imagination of the nation. It occupied newspaper headlines for months, involved dozens of officers, a police dog, helicopter, and numerous road closures whenever tips were received of possible sightings.

And the tips were plentiful as the public fastened onto the story and devoured the updates like people today binge-watch a true crime series. There were alleged sightings across the province and as far away as Nanaimo and Victoria, BC, but most led to dead ends.

A farmer in Stonewall reported one of his cows had been milked in the pasture. A woman near Argyle said a man matching Moggey's description asked for a drink of water. An engineer at the Wilkes Avenue pumping station in Winnipeg said he saw a man run into bushes near the plant.

And roadblocks were set up near Nipigon, northeast of Port Arthur, to check cars after reports that Moggey had been seen hitchhiking. Even the FBI in the United States was on the lookout as far as Miami, Florida.

The 5-foot-6, 160-pound Moggey remained under the radar for nearly eleven months—nine months longer than any other Manitoba escapee.

"For two days farmers have watched police cars racing up and down the country roads, stopping all vehicles. Scores of tips have been checked from the area and each one has proved disappointing," the July 27, 1960, *Winnipeg Free Press* reported, noting about thirty officers were on the case.

But the 5-foot-6, 160-pound Moggey remained under the radar for nearly eleven months—nine months longer than any other Manitoba escapee.

And his legend grew.

World War with the US Army, Robbins opens his own ice cream shop, Snowbird Ice Cream, in December 1945.

The owner of a men's clothing store in Chicago, Burton Baskin, marries Robbins's sister in 1942 and the couple moves to California in 1946. Robbins talks Baskin into selling ice cream rather than shirts and ties. Burton's Ice Cream opens in Pasadena later that year.

In 1948, there are five Snowbird stores and three Burton's stores. The brothers-in-law create a single company to operate them but find themselves stretched thin trying to oversee them all. They sell them to the individual managers—with an agreement on how they would be operated—becoming the first food company to franchise their outlets.

In 1953, they rebrand the head company and stores as Baskin-Robbins, relying on a coin toss to decide the naming order.

The ice cream empire has about 500 stores when it is sold to United Fruit Company in 1967 for an estimated $12 million.

Six months later, Burt Baskin dies of a heart attack. Robbins stays with the company until 1978. When he retires, the company is selling 20 million

As the public's appetite deepened for more information on the fugitive, his past was dragged onto the newspaper pages, recounting crimes committed by the man whose aliases included James O'Brien, Percy O'Brien, Pat Martin, and George Hamilton.

CRIMINAL LIFE

Moggey was born in 1904 near Portage la Prairie, west of Winnipeg, and grew up in Gypsumville, a small community on the north bank of Lake St. Martin in Manitoba's Interlake Region. He was introduced to crime at an early age. His dad was a horse trader who allegedly once bought an old, scrawny mare, fattened it up, painted its face and legs, and resold it at a higher price to the person he bought it from, according to the book, *Over the Prison Wall: The Story of Percy Moggey*, by John Warms.

At nineteen, Moggey was sentenced to eighteen months in the Dauphin jail after being charged for selling homebrew just before Prohibition ended in the province. He broke out of the jail in December and escalated his lawlessness.

In St. James, then a city of its own and now a Winnipeg neighbourhood, he stole a racehorse and a team of workhorses, along with harnesses, which he sold to a farmer. He later broke into a store at Oak Point in the Interlake and was nearly caught by police but escaped under gunfire. Moggey made his way to the United States and hid out in Milwaukee before returning to Manitoba at the start of summer 1924.

The twenty-year old rounded up five people—one as young as eleven—and the gang left a trail of crimes. They robbed a store and stole a truck in Westbourne then made their way to Portage la Prairie where they broke into railway cars and stole goods, then hit up a milling company and the Portage la Prairie Cream Company.

BANK SHOOTOUT

The crime spree culminated in Winnipeg on July 10 in a gun battle that left two police detectives wounded and Moggey with a bullet through his knee.

Moggey entered the Bank of Commerce at Alexander Avenue and Main Street shortly before closing time that afternoon. He handed over some Swiss currency for exchange. The foreign currency had been stolen four days earlier when Moggey and his gang robbed a brokerage office two blocks away at Main and Henry Avenue.

The crime spree culminated in Winnipeg on July 10 in a gun battle that left two police detectives wounded and Moggey with a bullet through his knee.

The Winnipeg Evening Tribune

THE WEATHER
Temperature—At 7 o'clock, 72; at noon, 74. Thursday's maximum, 83; minimum, 48.
Sun Above Horizon—15 hrs. 4 min. Sunrise, 4.31 a.m. Sunset, 8.35 p.m. Moonrise, 12.4 o'clock. Moonset, 8.22 o'clock.

VOL. XXXV.   WINNIPEG, FRIDAY, JULY 11, 1924 —18 PAGES   Price 5 Cents; With Comics, 10 Cents.   No. 167

FIVE ARRESTS FOLLOW MAIN ST. GUNFIGHT

MOTHER'S SINS SEND PRINCE TO BECOME PRIEST

Elopement of Queen Louise 21 Years Ago Ends With Son in Robes

FORMER ROYAL CONSORT NOW HUMBLE TEACHER

[Special Cable to the Winnipeg Tribune]
(Copyright, 1924)

BERLIN, July 11.—Former Crown Prince George of Saxony will embrace the priesthood in the mediaeval cloister of Trepnitz next Tuesday to expiate the sins of his mother.

Twenty-one years ago, the then Queen Louise, consort of Frederick August, fled in the dawn from her Dresden palace. She left her four children, for the passionate love of a fiery-souled Italian pianist, Toraelli, a second-rate artist, who later posed in low cafes in Florence and banked on his notoriety as a Don Juan.

Frederick divorced his wife, but a child was born two months after she left him. The scandal of the flight gave way to a battle over the parentage of the child. Finally the King acknowledged her as the Princess Monaco, but the mother he cast off forever.

Scores Dissipation

George, now 21, has lived from childhood under the shadow of the scandal and branded nearly all his life.

Flying Scotch Parson Wins 400 Metres—New Record

Liddell Shatters Mark Set by American Flash in Trials Canadian Gets 4th Place

Fitch, Hailed as World-beater, Forced to Relinquish Victory to Briton—Canada goes from Last Place to Eighth In Standing.

[By Canadian Press]

OLYMPIC STADIUM, Colombes, July 11.— Eric H. Liddell, the British flying parson, crowned himself Olympic 400 metre champion this afternoon in the world's record time of 47⅗ seconds, defeating Horatio Fitch, United States, who had shattered the previous world's record an hour before in the semi-finals.

Total Imposing

The victory of Liddell in the one metre run, today's only final event, was the British total as an imposing third among the point scores.

Canada, which began the day's competition at the bottom of the list of point-scoring nations, rose to eighth place through the prowess of D. M. Johnson, Montreal Rhodes scholar, who came fourth in the 400-metre race, and added three points to the Canadian total.

Canada is tied with South Africa in the point score and leads New Zealand.

The point score follows:

United States, 133½; Finland, 100; Great Britain, 60½; Sweden, 24 1-5; France, 13½; Switzerland, 11; Hungary, 11; Canada, 5; South Africa, 5; Norway, 4; New Zealand, 4; Denmark, 3½.

"I MUST HAVE DOPE," ADDICT SAYS IN COURT

Witness Says He Would be Maniac or Dead in 48 Hours if Supply Cut Off

"If my supply of dope were cut off, in 48 hours I'd either be a raving maniac or dead," a drug addict declared in provincial court Thursday.

AIDED POLICE TO GET BANDIT

WILFORD B. TURNER

IT was in great measure due to the nerve and speed of Mr. Turner that Detective Frayne was able to effect the capture of Percy Moggey, desperate gunman, Thursday afternoon. With the detective severely wounded, and with bullets whizzing through the air behind Liggett's cigar store at Logan and Main sts., Mr. Turner rushed into the lane, stopping with the gunman, and held him while the injured officer handcuffed him. "Moggey put up a grand fight," Mr. Turner said. Mr. Turner is an employe of the Liggett firm.

PENSION BONUS PERMANENCY IS ASKED IN REPORT

Raise in Grant of $300 Per Year Advocated by House Committee

MERITORIOUS CLAUSE ALSO IS UNDER CONSIDERATION

[By Canadian Press]

OTTAWA, July 11.—That the existing pension bonus of 50 percent be absorbed into the basic pension rate, thereby making the increase in the rate of pension for single, totally disabled men, from $600 to $900, is recommended by the House committee on soldiers' pension, in its third report, tabled in the House today.

The committee concurs for the most part with the recommendations of the royal commission on pensions and re-establishment in regard to legislation affecting ex-soldiers and their dependents.

The report recommends that the meritorious clause, which provides for grants to be "specially meritorious" such cases having the approval of the governor-general-in-council.

WHERE GUNFIGHT STARTED

THE crowd gathered around the Alexander street branch of the Canadian Bank of Commerce Thursday afternoon just after the gun battle in which two detectives and a bandit were wounded.

Above at the right is detective Frayne, shot through the abdomen. Lower left is Fred Batho, shot through the shoulder. The captured bandit, Percy Moggey, was hit in the knee. Both detectives are recovering.

POLICE DECLARE PERCY MOGGEY IS GANG LEADER

Arrests Will End Long Chapter of Crimes in City, Police Say

WOUNDED DETECTIVES ARE MAKING RECOVERY

The condition of Detectives Frayne and Batho, as well as Moggey, all confined to the Winnipeg General hospital, was reported to be entirely satisfactory early this afternoon.

The work of the two detectives was highly commended by Chief of Detectives George Smith. Batho has been with the department 29 years and Frayne about 15. The double arrest and courage of the two wounded officers was a source of admiration by other members of the force today.

In the hospital today Detective Batho made light of his trouble saying "well, the main thing is that we got the man."

Their bandit leader is a police-guarded ward of the General hospital with a bullet through his knee, five young men, alleged followers of Percy Moggey, gunman and desperado, who late Thursday afternoon wounded two detectives in a fight on Main st. are in the city cells today.

The five were gathered in the different late yesterday, after the big battle, and a long string of charges are hanging over them.

Newspaper headline after shootout on Main Street *THE WINNIPEG EVENING TRIBUNE, JULY 11, 1924 P.1*

Banks had been put on alert for anyone trying to pass foreign bills, so the teller stalled Moggey, saying she had to confirm the exchange rate. She tracked down her manager, who called police

while telling Moggey he was phoning the bank's head office to find out the value.

Detectives Fred Batho and Robert Frayne raced to the bank and confronted Moggey, asking where he got the money. Moggey said he had just come from overseas and brought it with him. The detectives said he needed to go with them to the police station so they could verify his claims. Moggey slipped his hand into his pocket and backed away. Batho demanded he remove his hand and Moggey yanked it out, holding a revolver. He fired at the detective, who was struck in the chest. Batho dropped and his shirt filled with blood.

Frayne charged at Moggey, and the two men crashed through a swinging door into the space behind the tellers' counter, falling to the floor. As clerks ran, so did Moggey, leaping over Frayne and out the main door. Frayne got up and gave chase.

Moggey ran north on Main, turning to fire at Frayne, who shot back. Moggey rounded the corner onto Logan Avenue and headed up an alley that dead-ended at the back of Liggett's Drug Store.

Cornered, Moggey turned and fired again at Frayne, who shot a fraction of a second sooner. Frayne's bullet struck the right knee of Moggey, who flinched as he pulled his trigger. The shot, originally aimed at Frayne's chest, instead struck

gallons of ice cream every year in more than 2,000 stores around the world.

1918
Alice Edith Ostrander, who lost her vision at an early age, is appointed by the Canadian National Institute for the Blind as the first home teacher for the blind in Western Canada. She used a knitting machine to knit 14,000 pairs of socks and leggings for the troops during the First World War, which earned her a special commendation from the Prince of Wales.

1919
May 15: The largest strike in Canadian history, the Winnipeg General Strike, begins with some 30,000 workers walking off their jobs.

The Winnipeg Trades and Labour Council had appealed for a general strike to support the city's building and metal workers, who had been striking since May 1 for better wages, better working conditions and the right to collective bargaining.

Officially, it is set to begin at 11 a.m. but the first to make an impact are the Hello Girls—women telephone operators. When their 7 a.m. shift starts, their desks remain empty. At 11 a.m. the streets are flooded by the first wave of workers. Eventually, the strike involves an estimated 30,000 people—workers and others who joined in solidarity. Over the next six weeks, economic activity grinds to a halt and the city becomes a focus of international attention.

It all culminates with a violent clash on Bloody Saturday, June 21, and quietly ends five days later. By the time it is over, two men are killed, and thousands of impoverished people lose their jobs as the effort does not win the strikers any

concessions. At least not immediately.

The spirit of the movement gives birth to a unified labour movement and social democratic politics, but it takes three decades for employers to recognize unions and grant collective bargaining rights.

September: Winnipeg's Earl Grey School becomes the first junior high school in Canada.

The three-storey building, which opened in 1915, contains 29 classrooms, five special classrooms, and an assembly hall. That offers it space in 1919 to try something that hasn't yet been attempted in

Earl Grey School as seen in 1914   WINNIPEG SCHOOL DIVISION

Canada—revamping the curriculum and introducing a distinct middle-school experience.

The hope is to reduce the number of school dropouts by offering elective courses and rotating classes in specialized rooms.

The program, headed by superintendent Daniel McIntyre, is based on similar experiments in the United States. Standard educational practice at the time is eight years of elementary school followed by three or four years of

"Moggey's gunfight with detectives yesterday was one of the most spectacular in Winnipeg police annals." *Winnipeg Evening Tribune*

the detective just above his hip. Frayne staggered back and dropped his gun.

The battle was described to newspapers by a Liggett's employee who heard the initial gunshots as the men were running on Main. He came out and followed the chase into the alley.

After being hit, Frayne lurched at Moggey and grabbed hold of Moggey's revolver with both hands. The Liggett's employee leapt at Moggey with a flying tackle around the knees.

Moggey fought "like a fiend," according to the story in the *Winnipeg Evening Tribune*. Moggey and the employee were heaved across the alley into a garbage barrel. Frayne managed to get handcuffs onto one of Moggey's wrists just as reinforcements came charging up the alley.

Frayne and Batho were rushed to hospital while Moggey was first taken to the central police station, then to the hospital.

"Moggey's gunfight with detectives yesterday was one of the most spectacular in Winnipeg police annals," the *Tribune* reported.

PUBLIC SPANKING

As for the other members of the Moggey's gang who had helped with the earlier break-ins and robberies, two were arrested a few days before the shootout after they were found at Winnipeg's Empress Hotel and charged. Three more were rounded up in the hours after the shooting and were also charged in connection with the robberies, including the one at the brokerage. But Moggey, police said, acted alone at the Bank of Commerce.

His gang members were given a range of punishments, from three years in jail to suspended

high school. But many educators feel the shift to high school is too sudden. The Earl Grey experiment sets a six-year elementary period, followed by three years of departmentalized schooling—junior high—offering a range of subjects and electives and activities. Three years of high school follow that.

It is believed the middle school program will help reveal special skills or interests in students and prepare them for greater specialization in high school.

The experience is hugely successful. Lord Roberts and Lord Selkirk schools soon follow. By 1923 the program is in schools throughout the division. By 1925, it is in practice citywide and by 1935, nationwide.

The first school in Winnipeg purposely built as a junior high school is Isaac Newton, which opens in January 1922.

Earl Grey alumni include former Winnipeg Mayor Robert Steen, media philosopher Marshall McLuhan, musician Neil Young, former governor of The Bank of Canada James Elliott Coyne and deputy governor John Robert Beattie. The signatures of the latter two are featured on all Canadian paper currency between 1955 and 1961.

1920

October 15-17: The first paying passenger flight in Canada occurs in 1920, between Winnipeg and The Pas.

The journey of 625 kilometres takes nearly three days—53 hours—though the actual time in the air is six hours and 12 minutes.

Its impact, though, is still being felt.

Pilot Hector Dougall and mechanic Frank Ellis are the first people ever to fly north of the 53rd parallel, helping launch the era of bush pilots in the North. Their feat also shows commercial air travel is possible in Canada.

The world's first scheduled passenger flight happened six years earlier, January 1, 1914, in Florida. The 27-kilometre flight across the bay from St. Petersburg to Tampa Bay took about 23 minutes—about the same amount of time it now takes to drive between the two centres, around the bay, for 38 kilometres. But back then, the flight was 90 minutes quicker than by car.

The aviation industry is still in its infancy since Wilbur and Orville Wright made their historical flight at Kitty Hawk, North Carolina, in December 1903. But its development

sentences with no time served. In the latter cases, the judge decided the boys had been led astray by Moggey and deserved a fresh start.

The eleven-year-old bandit was sentenced to a vigorous public spanking by his mom, in lieu of one year in the Portage Training School—a youth correctional facility that offered work training in several trades (later renamed the Manitoba Home for Boys and then the Agassiz Youth Centre before it was shut down in July 2022).

"The drubbing was given with a heavy rubber strap while the entire police force looked on," according to the *Winnipeg Evening Tribune* of July 18, 1924.

Another member, a fifteen-year-old boy described by the judge as "a graduate in criminal work," was sentenced to three years and eighteen lashes, while a third one was given a year in the training school and twelve lashes.

It wasn't until July 28 that Moggey was discharged from hospital and set to appear in court August 1. Both detectives were still convalescing at home, Frayne doing much better than Batho, who would live the remainder of his life with a bullet in his left lung. Doctors worried he could lose the use of his left arm if they tried removing it.

Moggey was sentenced to ten years in prison for the shootings and twenty other crimes. During the sentencing, the judge offered a stern warning: "Do not try to escape, for you will not succeed. The world is too small for you to hide from the long arm of the law. You will be sought out from the uttermost parts of the earth and brought back."

During the sentencing, the judge offered a stern warning: "Do not try to escape, for you will not succeed. The world is too small for you to hide from the long arm of the law."

It was advice Moggey would not heed.

In 1930, Moggey tried to break out but was caught and given another year for his failed effort and for assaulting an officer when he was caught. He was released in 1934, but his freedom was fleeting. He went to Toronto in 1935 and went on a crime spree in the downtown, breaking into several stores with some partners. Police increased their surveillance of the area and one night they found the group suspiciously loitering in the wee hours of the night. Moggey and the others ran through alleys to dodge the police but came face to face with some cops in a cruiser. It led to a gun battle and more running. Moggey wounded two officers but was shot in the foot, slowing his escape effort. Once his gun was empty, he was an easy catch for other officers who arrived on scene. For these crimes he was sent to Kingston Penitentiary on a thirteen-year sentence. He tried to escape in 1937 but was caught and given another two years. He was released in 1947, but again his freedom was brief. In 1948 he was caught in Port Arthur with break-in tools and explosives, which netted him a four-year term at Stony Mountain. That was extended in 1949 by a three-year concurrent sentence after an escape that lasted just two hours.

A fellow inmate had swiped a small knife from the prison's shoemaker shop. This knife was later used to steal a truck as the inmate pressed it against the neck of a guard and forced him out of the vehicle. The inmate drove to the prison's pig farm where Moggey was working. Moggey, now 45, jumped into the passenger seat and the men sped out the prison gate.

The vehicle was found abandoned a short distance away. Because of Moggey's history of violence against police and the other inmate's use of a weapon against the guard, the search party took no chances. The pursuit was described at the time as one of the most intensive and heavily armed manhunts in the province's history.

The escapees were discovered lying in the cover of tall grass and brush about fourteen kilometres from the penitentiary. Police fired a pair of shots above their heads and the two men gave themselves up without a fight.

Moggey's hard life left him with a scar on the left side of his nose, a bent pinky finger on his right hand, and bullet scars on his foot and right knee. But after his release in 1953, it seemed Moggey had gone straight. He kept a low profile, and as four years passed, his name vanished from the headlines.

That is, until his frequent-guest card for Stony was stamped again in 1957. That was for the incident at Port Arthur that earned him the ten-year stay.

HIDDEN CABIN

When he flew the coop using the meat hook and pole in 1960, Moggey's myth took off.

Immediately after he fled from the prison, he scampered through bush and pasture, crawled through culverts and then stole a horse from a farmyard near Stonewall, which is where he found the cow to milk. He rode the horse for some distance, finding his way to Meadow Lea, 35 kilometres west of Stony Mountain. There, he tied

steadily grows to where cargo planes are carrying light loads between Ottawa and Montreal in 1913.

The First World War propels the industry forward as planes became a new weapon. But following the war, most Canadians see no use for the flying in peacetime, viewing them only as a military venture.

By 1920, a handful of airline companies in Canada are giving barnstorming demonstrations—exhibitions of flying and aeronautical stunts—but none are flying passengers between destinations. One barnstorming company is Winnipeg-based Canadian Aircraft Co. That's where Dougall and Ellis are working when Frank J. Stanley, a fur buyer from The Pas, walks in and asks to be flown home.

Automobile use is growing at the time but most of the paved roads are in cities and towns. The routes elsewhere are cart paths carved through dirt. A journey to The Pas would have to be done by horseback or buggy and take several days through raw bush and bog.

Dougall and Ellis pack up and get set to take Stanley, despite the route being unfamiliar and almost completely across

Biplane Avro 504-K seen in front of The Pas Lumber Co., in 1920, during the first passenger flight in Canada SAM WALLER MUSEUM/ ELIZABETH KILOH COLLECTION PP96.2.21

wilderness. To top it off, their Avro 504K biplane has an open cockpit and limited cruising range.

The two-seater was purchased from the British government after the war and converted into a three-seater. The trio depart Winnipeg at 11 a.m. and intend to reach Dauphin before refuelling. But around Gladstone, a spark plug begins to misfire, and the plane is forced to land in a field.

The plug is replaced and soon the plane is back in the air. In Dauphin they find another field to land and take a two-hour layover to fuel the plane and themselves. The next stop is Swan River, where they hike from yet another field to a hotel to spend the night.

The plan for the next day is to follow the Hudson Bay Railway line, which veers into Saskatchewan before turning back into Manitoba and on to The Pas. Clouds and snow squalls force them at times to fly much lower than they want to keep the railway tracks in view.

By the time they reach Hudson Bay Junction, Saskatchewan, the plane has swallowed nearly half its fuel fighting the head-winds. Dougall decides to land but needs to circle several times to find a clearing in the thick bush. He finally locates a patch of muskeg, prays it isn't too soft, and aims the plane's nose toward it. The wheels sink axle-deep, creating a jarring stop, but the mud is otherwise cold enough to support them.

Several people come out to see the machine and help free the axles. They then begin clearing a make-shift runway to a nearby rise, according to an article by historian Bruce Cherney.

It takes until the after-noon of the next day for the

the horse to a tree where someone would find it and hopped a flatcar as a westbound train slowed through the village.

As police were putting an "iron ring" around the Stonewall area due to the cow-milking incident, Moggey was on his way to Brandon. Just outside that city, he hitchhiked a lift north with the manager of Dauphin's Woolworths store. The man was heading back to that city, north of Riding Mountain National Park.

Moggey, who was still wearing grey prison-issued coveralls, purported to be a house painter heading there for work. So the man offered him a job painting his own house. Following through with his lie, Moggey started the job one morning, but never finished. When the man went to check the house at noon, Moggey was long gone, never to return. A couple of days later the man realized who

He wandered the rest of the summer, pumping water from farmyards and stealing food where he could.

he had picked up and called police, describing Moggey as "quiet-spoken and pleasant."

As police flooded the Dauphin area, more leads came in. A truck driver said he gave Moggey a ride to Ashville Junction, west of Dauphin, while a woman said she was driving near the north gate of Riding Mountain when a man matching Moggey's description stopped her to ask about the park's boundary line.

Roadblocks were set up as far north as The Pas and west to the Saskatchewan border. As the police were getting closer in August, Moggey caught a break: Scout, a police tracking dog, went on leave to get his tonsils removed.

Once again, Moggey slipped through the police dragnet and made his way back to the other side of Lake Manitoba. He wandered the rest of the summer, pumping water from farmyards and

runway to be cut through the bush. The generosity of the villagers saves the journey. Their hard work not only involves the runway work, but also the gathering of cans of fuel, as no other supplies are available. The slap-dash runway is just wide enough, and Dougall's skill keeps the biplane's lower wings just slashing across the tops of the trees.

The gathered fuel is enough to complete the final 140 kilometres to The Pas, where the men spot a cow pasture a few blocks east of town and make their descent. A civic banquet is held to celebrate the pioneering event and to welcome the first passenger to the North.

The return flight to Winnipeg is far less adventuresome: Dougall and Ellis dismantle the plane and ship it on the rail line.

1922
February: The first issue of *Reader's Digest* is published.

It is co-founded by Lila Bell Acheson Wallace and her husband DeWitt Wallace. Acheson was born in Virden, Manitoba. Her dad was a minister who relocated the family to the United States when she was a child, and she grew up in Minnesota and Illinois.

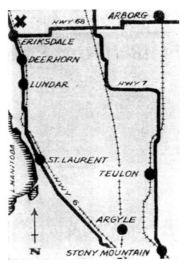

An X marks the spot (top left corner) where Moggey's hideout was located just north of Eriksdale. *THE WINNIPEG TRIBUNE, JUNE 12, 1961, P.4*

stealing food where he could. When the fall breezes arrived, he set about finding shelter.

At the end of a narrow dirt-and-gravel path that became swallowed by aspen groves, about six kilometres north of Eriksdale, Moggey found an isolated spot that would become his hideout. About two kilometres off the path, along an even narrower trail, Moggey cut down trees and built a small cabin from hand-hewn logs.

He had worked in lumber camps during his four years between prison stints and knew how to live in the bush. He completed his cabin—including the door and bedframe—over the course of one week in September, using tools pilfered from properties in the area. He later said he chose the spot because it was far enough from farms and towns that he thought he would be isolated.

The Interlake is shaped by shallow lakes and ponds, stretched out like a smudged drawing. Even the expanses of forest and cattail marshes slant the same way, carved by the last glaciation as the ice retreated.

Lawrence Swan, one of the men who helped lead police to Moggey's hideout, stands in the doorway of the cabin.

UNIVERSITY OF WINNIPEG ARCHIVES, WESTERN CANADA PICTORIAL INDEX/*WINNIPEG TRIBUNE* COLLECTION A0828-24773

Moggey also found enough tree cover for camouflage, which he supplemented by transplanting some shrubs and smaller trees to thicken the screen. He found a woodstove at an abandoned farm and carried it, and the stovepipes, through the bush over the course of a day back to his shack. And he found a .22 calibre rifle he used for hunting rabbits and partridge. He cut the barrel back to make it easier to carry and whittled the handle into a pistol grip. He also stole batteries and a transistor radio, which he hung from the wall near his bed and listened, with amusement, to reports about the search for him.

It likely helped that the only photo available showed Moggey with a receding hairline but otherwise fairly thick, dark hair. In the five or so years since, he had become quite bald and any remaining hair had turned grey.

"Once I listened to a broadcast which said I had bummed a meal out in Vancouver. It was really funny," Moggey later told the *Free Press*.

Despite being under such a spotlight, he was able to go undetected even when he ventured into civilization.

"Once in a while I took tours to keep myself occupied," he told the newspaper, explaining how he walked to towns around the area, stopping for beer at pubs and breaking into businesses to take a little cash or food—a can of beans here and there, not enough to raise suspicion or bring out the law.

It likely helped, police would later say, that the only photo available showed Moggey with a receding hairline but otherwise fairly thick, dark hair. In the five or so years since, he had become quite bald and any remaining hair had turned grey.

There were times Moggey rushed out to extinguish small forest fires ignited by lightning, both to prevent anyone else from coming out and to preserve his woodland cover. When the snow arrived, he spent most of his time near his stove and radio, surviving on stolen food and on animals he shot. In mid-February 1961, the elusive Moggey was declared one of Canada's five most wanted criminals.

First *Reader's Digest*,
February 1922, Vol. 1 No. 1.

By 1929, the New York-based magazine had 290,000 subscribers and an annual gross income of $900,000. The first international edition was published in the United Kingdom in 1938. By the time the magazine turned forty, it had forty international editions in thirteen languages and Braille, and a total circulation of 23 million.

Reader's Digest was the best-selling consumer magazine in the United States until 2009, when it was passed by *Better Homes and Gardens*. In late 2023, Trusted Media Brand, the current US-based publisher announced it was ceasing its Canadian operations as it struggled against declining revenue.

April 3: The first radio broadcast from the first private broadcast radio licence in Canada takes place.

The station, CJCG, is owned by the *Manitoba Free Press* (renamed *Winnipeg Free Press* in 1931). The *Winnipeg Tribune* follows up on April 20 with its own radio station.

Radio fever also sweeps up the city's two major theatres, the Capitol and the Allen, both of which install receivers and large speakers, and advertise reception from stations in Boston, Pittsburgh, and San Francisco. It's an attraction because movies with sound are still seven years away. Still, the radio experiment is a bit of a bust for the theatres. They end it after just a few weeks.

CJCG is believed to be the first station to ever live broadcast an entire hockey game when it features the Winnipeg Falcons against Port Arthur at the Winnipeg Amphitheatre on February 22, 1923. But not long after, later the same year, the newspapers shut down their stations. They give up their licences to the Manitoba government so the Manitoba Telephone System can get into broadcasting, creating CKY radio (Winnipeg) and CKX radio (Brandon).

December 30: The technology that made TV, movies, and the fax machine possible, is patented by a Winnipegger who becomes a wartime spymaster.

Sir William Stephenson is best known as the inspiration for Ian Fleming's James Bond character, but the Winnipeg native was also an inventor who created a radiofacsimile device, radiofax, that enabled the wireless transmission of photographs. His wirephoto would help revolutionize the newspaper industry and is still in limited use for transmitting weather charts and information to ships at sea.

William Samuel Clouston Stanger was born January 23, 1897, (many reports have his birthdate as January 11, 1896, but Vital Statistics lists the 1897 date). His last name was changed to Stephenson after his father died in 1901.

His mother was left with three kids—an infant, a two-year-old, and four-year-old William—and little money. She turned to friends, Kristin and Vigfus Stephenson, who raised William in their home on Syndicate Street in Winnipeg's Point Douglas area.

The teenage Stephenson was fascinated with radio and tinkered with transmitters and receivers, electricity, and steam engines. He even rigged

William Stephenson with wireless photo transmitter he invented, 1922 CIA/CIA.GOV

up his own Morse code telegraph and tapped out messages to ships on the Great Lakes.

In December 1913 Stephenson helped capture John "Bloody Jack" Krafchenko, a bank

CAPTURE AND A CUPPA

Despite all his care and caution to remain a hidden hermit, it was a fluke encounter that brought Moggey's residency of just over nine months in the bush to an end.

Three men from the Lake Manitoba First Nation were picking Seneca roots in the area one Friday afternoon in early June 1961. The plant was used by Indigenous communities to treat coughs and colds and is still used in the preparation of commercial cough syrup and cough drops.

The men stumbled across Moggey's cabin, and he opened the door. They all chatted by the doorway for about ten minutes, during which Moggey questioned them about Seneca and claimed he was trapping muskrats.

When the men left, they thought it strange that someone living in the area wasn't aware of Seneca and was trapping an animal uncommon for the region. According to Statistics Canada, Manitoba once accounted for 80 per cent of the total Canadian export of Seneca root, which was most plentiful in the Interlake.

robber and killer hiding in Winnipeg. Stephenson was delivering telegrams for the Great North Western Telegraph company when he spotted the wanted man and notified police.

During his arrest, Krafchenko told police his fountain pen was filled with explosive nitroglycerine. Apparently, the police weren't overly concerned as they poured out the liquid, which they said looked like regular ink, into a sink. But the story, and Krafchenko's disguises while on the lam, captured Stephenson's imagination and would influence his future spy career.

In 1916, he joined the Royal Canadian Engineers and was sent to France during the First World War. He later joined the Royal Flying Corps and became an ace pilot, shooting down twenty-six planes. He was wounded and captured in 1918 but managed to escape, then filed a report on German prison camps that aided British intelligence forces.

William Stephenson's stolen Sieger German can opener THE INTREPID SOCIETY/INTREPID-SOCIETY.ORG

Back in Winnipeg after the war, Stephenson launched a business based on a German can opener he stole from his prisoner camp. He was impressed with the smooth edge it left on an opened tin and marketed it as Kleen Kut. He formed a business partnership with a friend to sell the device, along with other cutlery and hardware. But it was a difficult time with the economy struggling, and the partners filed for bankruptcy in 1922.

Stephenson returned to London, where fortune struck—several times. He perfected his work on wirephoto, which he first designed as a student at the University of Manitoba and patented it that same year. Soon after, the *Daily Mail* published the world's first wire photo and within five years Stephenson was a millionaire.

He spread his money and interests, buying a controlling interest in the General Radio Company and beginning to manufacture popular low-cost radios.

He became owner of an aircraft manufacturer that developed a plane that evolved into the Spitfire, which became the most famous plane of the Second World War.

Stephenson was also involved in the plastics, steel, and concrete industries. And he foresaw the development of TV, believing moving images could be transferred through a light-sensitive device, like his wirephoto fax, if the rate of transmission was sped up.

"Moving pictures … may soon be possible to see … at one's home," he once said.

He coined the term tele-vision and wrote papers with mathematical equations to prove his theory. He established Sound City films and built Shepperton Studios, which eventually became the largest film studio outside Hollywood.

William Stephenson passport photo, 1942 WIKIMEDIA COMMONS

Through it all, he made friends in high places and developed a large circle of business contacts. It was through them that Stephenson learned in the 1930s about the buildup of German armaments and the Enigma coding device. He tried to warn the British government but some within were anti-Semitic

The men took their suspicions to the RCMP in Lundar later that evening. The RCMP officer on duty, Const. Paul Hughes, showed them a photo of Moggey, and they were certain it was the same man in the bush.

Hughes contacted his superior, Cpl. Grant Russell, who was in Winnipeg at the time. When Russell got back it was dark, so he decided to wait until morning to have the men lead him to Moggey's cabin.

Everyone slept overnight on the detachment's jail cots. They were joined in the morning of June 10 by the MLA for the area, Elman Guttormson, who was also a *Free Press* reporter and later wrote an award-winning story about the capture.

The six men reached Moggey's place around 5 a.m. Hughes aimed his revolver on a rear window while Russell readied his .303 rifle and kicked in the door, yelling for Moggey to step out. Guttormson held a .22 rifle nearby, and the men from Lake Manitoba remained some distance back.

Wearing his coveralls and blinking in the light, the stocky Moggey sleepily stepped out like a

REPORTER AIDS POSSE

Police Capture Percy Moggey

Stony Mountain Fugitive Nabbed

In Hideout Near Eriksdale

By ELMAN GUTTORMSON
Free Press Reporter

An armed posse of two RCMP officers, and this reporter captured Percy Moggey this morning.

One officer guarded the rear of a bush-buried shack, four miles north of Eriksdale, Man., I stood to the side, and Cpl. Grant Russell of the Lundar RCMP detachment kicked in the door.

A man in grey coveralls and socks, obviously wakened from sleep by the 5 a.m. knock at his door, stumbled out, hands in the air. He looked at the guns and grinned — "You can put those away," he said.

See photos of capture scene. Page 54

"You're Moggey, aren't you?" asked Cpl. Russell.

"Yes," came the clear reply.

So the man who was the first prisoner ever to go "over the wall" at Stony Mountain — a criminal who had shot and wounded four police officers in his career, and the man who stayed free after his escape longer than anyone else in Manitoba, was once more in custody.

First of all, I would like to get one thing clear. I was a member of the posse, armed with a .22 rifle, only as a helper. The police officers did the original investigation, made the arrest, and did all the work. I watched.

Elman Guttormson re-enacts the capture of Percy Moggey.
WINNIPEG FREE PRESS, JUNE 10, 1961 P.1

Khru Wi Neg

Told Kenned

Issue Open

PALM BEACH,
S. Khrushchev told P
Vienna last weekend
was concerned, not a
to negotiation, it's le

groundhog forced out in February. After eluding police for ten months and fifteen days, the fight was gone.

"You can put those away," the 57-year-old said about the guns, holding his hands up.

He was ordered to take the coveralls off to be searched for weapons. He had nothing else on but socks, and once the officers checked those, they let him relax and dress.

As Russell went into the cabin, Moggey pointed to his bed, saying the only thing of interest was under there. Russell lifted the mattress and found the sawed-off rifle as well as a silencer Moggey was making so he could hunt less conspicuously.

When he saw the men from Lake Manitoba, he said "I never thought these fellows would have recognized me or I would have taken off quick. I would have been twenty miles from here now."

Moggey offered everyone a cup of tea. They refused but let him enjoy one before he was escorted away.

He was taken to the Lundar detachment and guarded by three additional Mounties called in from Winnipeg, before being driven to Stonewall to be arraigned and finally returned to Stony.

"The capture of Moggey marked the end of a manhunt which, at times, involved dozens of police units throughout the continent."

Winnipeg Tribune, June 12, 1961.

"At no time during the arrest or on the trip to jail, and throughout his stay in Lundar, did Moggey offer any resistance or show any antagonism," the *Winnipeg Tribune* reported on June 12, 1961. "The capture of Moggey marked the end of a manhunt which, at times,

and actually sympathetic to Adolf Hitler. Others just didn't want to hear it as Britain was still recovering from the First World War.

A British MP named Winston Churchill was the only one who listened, and Stephenson continued to supply Churchill with intelligence.

When Churchill became Prime Minister in 1940, he sent Stephenson to New York to direct the US-based British Security Coordination (BSC) and enlist the United States as an ally in the war. The telegraphic address of the BSC in New York was INTREPID, which also became Stephenson's wartime code name. He coordinated all British overseas espionage activities in the Western Hemisphere, recruited agents, and established a secret base, Camp X, in Whitby, Ontario., to train agents for espionage missions behind enemy lines. It is believed to be the first training school for wartime operations in North America.

Around two thousand British, Canadian, and American covert operators were trained in Whitby from 1941 to 1945. Among them were future famous authors Roald Dahl and Ian Fleming. Fleming told *The Times* newspaper in London in 1961 that "James

Statue of Sir William Stephenson on Memorial Boulevard
DARREN BERNHARDT

Bond is a highly romanticized version of a true spy. The real thing is …William Stephenson."

Stephenson was considered the single most powerful intelligence operative in the Western

Hemisphere. In New York, his official title was British Passport Control Officer. But the BSC's activities ranged from censoring transatlantic mail, breaking letter codes, forging diplomatic documents, obtaining military codes, and protecting American factories producing munitions for Britain.

He also served as liaison between the BSC and the US government until the Office of Strategic Services (OSS) assumed responsibility for US intelligence in 1942. Stephenson was instrumental in helping to establish the OSS, which later developed into the CIA.

His intelligence network is credited with deciphering Enigma, an accomplishment said to have helped end the war earlier, by as much as six months, and save many lives.

He was knighted in 1945 and died on January 31, 1989.

A statue of Stephenson, created by Leo Mol, stands on Winnipeg's Memorial Boulevard, watching over the legislative building. Smaller replicas of the statue are in places around the world, including Buckingham Palace and the CIA museum in Virginia.

1925
November 15: The Royal Canadian Legion—or what would become it—is formed during a meeting at the Marlborough Hotel on Smith Street in downtown Winnipeg.

After the end of the First World War, numerous veterans' groups and associations form in Canada to provide support and advocate for former service members. Despite their common goal, the lack of unity leaves their efforts fragmented.

Representatives from several of the groups meet at the Marlborough and agree to amalgamate and form the Canadian Legion of the British Empire Services League. It is incorporated by an Act of Parliament the following year.

The organization, known more simply as the Canadian Legion, grows steadily during the 1930s and more rapidly after the Second World War, lobbying and advising the government for pension and health benefits for veterans.

In 1960, Queen Elizabeth II grants it royal patronage, and the name formally becomes the Royal Canadian Legion.

involved dozens of police units throughout the continent."

Within days of the police walking through the thick bush to Moggey's hideout, hundreds of people had been drawn to the site of the infamous fugitive.

"The virgin territory surrounding the area where Percy Moggey had built his cabin was transformed into a tourist Mecca shortly after news was released about the capture," the *Free Press* reported.

The dense bush was beaten into a wide path, with cars driving to within 100 metres of the cabin. The main road leading to the site was soon nicknamed Moggey's Road and later given the title officially by the municipality. The road is an extension of Eriksdale's Railway Avenue, changing names at a curve near a bygone intersection with Highway 6.

A week after his capture, Moggey had two more years tacked onto his original 1957 sentence.

ONE LAST TIME

He was released in 1967 but Moggey, being Moggey, couldn't help himself.

In August 1968, there was a break-in at the Original Pancake House on Pembina Highway in Winnipeg. Five men passing by just before 4 a.m. saw movement inside, so they pulled around back just as three figures dashed out with bags. The men gave chase but were only able to catch the slowest of the bunch—a 64-year-old Moggey who was slowed by arthritis.

The men told police he threatened to shoot them but when that bluff failed, he tried bargaining, offering them $80 to let him go. Police found break-in tools in Moggey's bag, and closer to the restaurant they recovered keyhole saws, a crowbar, and other break-in tools.

Moggey was a dishwasher at the Pancake House, and though he didn't have keys, he knew he could easily pick the locks. And he figured the robbery would be quick because he knew where everything was located inside.

Police escort Percy Moggey to court in June 1961.
THE WINNIPEG TRIBUNE, JUNE 16, 1961, P.1

Judge John Enns expressed reverence for Moggey, saying "I can't help feeling some admiration for having escaped detection for so long." But leniency wasn't served. Moggey got a return ticket for another four years in prison.

Moggey was released early, around 1970, to be cared for by family. He had suffered a stroke that left him partially paralyzed. On August 8, 1974, Moggey died in Winnipeg at age 69.

At the court hearing, Moggey's lawyer asked for leniency: "Now in the twilight of his life and the twilight of his career, he can no longer look forward to earning a living in a normal way. He is eligible for the (old age) pension next year. He merely stands before your worship and simply says, 'I'm an old man, I would like to spend the rest of my days in freedom.'"

REBUILT CABIN

The sweep of time eventually caused Moggey and his capers to fade into murky memories. It bleached the violence and made him a kind of folk hero to some. Others completely forgot about him, and new generations came along without ever hearing his name.

However, whenever winter wrought its extremes, a few of those who remembered the outlaw that endured those conditions in his hastily made hideout, would begin talking—and planning. The idea of making Moggey's cabin

The rebuilt Moggey's cabin from outside and inside, and the sign at the start of the path that leads to the site DARREN BERNHARDT

a tourist attraction took shape during those conversations inside an Eriksdale coffee shop in the mid-1990s. The problem was that there was no cabin anymore. Both time and looters had stolen it.

The idea of making Moggey's cabin a tourist attraction took shape in the mid-1990s. The problem was that there was no cabin anymore. Both time and looters had stolen it.

People hoping to find hidden money rifled through it in the months and early years after Moggey's capture, taking souvenirs, including parts of the structure itself. All that was left were some rotting logs. But there were photographs from the 1960s and the idea sprouted to make a

replica. Hours of volunteer labour, bush clearing and fundraising led to the start of construction in April 1998.

The three-by-four-metre replica opened to the public July 29, 2000, with a parking lot nearby—leaving a half-kilometre hike in. The reconstruction was sturdier to withstand the elements and was fashioned with items Moggey reportedly had—stove, washbasin, saw, axe, and lantern. But many of those have been taken by visitors in the years since.

Despite some initial backlash to the idea of venerating a career criminal, Warms, who was involved in the cabin replica, explained it this way to the *Free Press*: "It is against what all of us really believe in and yet it was such an intriguing phenomenon we felt it was worth doing something with…This is part of the history of the area."

Although clearly hotheaded, Moggey apparently spent his time between jail terms splurging on strangers, treating ladies to drinks in the bars and hanging candy in trees for kids to find.

During research for his book, Warms discovered Moggey had more than one hideout. He had also dug a cave—a man-sized gopher hole, as Warms called it—in a gravel ridge near Spearhill, about 55 kilometres north of the cabin. A narrow ramp led to a wooden door. The lack of a thick forest floor and undergrowth at that site proved more comfortable in the warmer months, as it allowed for more air movement. There was also a nearby den, camouflaged behind trees and branches, where Moggey would retreat and hide things if someone was approaching the cave.

He built a lookout in some treetops, which provided a vantage point from which he could see a good distance. To access it, he cleared a foot-wide space on the branches, which doubled as a ladder.

Nothing remains of those sites anymore.

"It is against what all of us really believe in and yet it was such an intriguing phenomenon we felt it was worth doing something with. This is part of the history of the area." John Warms

SECRETS OF THE CIVIC AUDITORIUM

The Manitoba Archives building is a time capsule in Art Deco style, clutching the stories of the province, its people and places. It takes up an entire downtown city block for its repository of history. Yet its own story—even its existence—is largely unknown.

The first surveys of the Red River Settlement and correspondences of Louis Riel are there, along with court records dating to 1835, the story behind the suffrage movement and how women in Manitoba became the first in Canada to win the right to vote, as well as maps and images of bygone times, buildings and streets, and filled-in creeks.

CANADIAN INDUSTRIAL EXHIBITION

Undated postcard of Civic Auditorium opening in 1932 INTERNET ARCHIVE

ABOVE LEFT Early sketch of proposed Golden Boy for the Manitoba legislative building, 1915. Included in a file of correspondence between Frank W. Simon, architect of the building, and French sculptor George Gardet. PROVINCIAL ARCHIVES OF MANITOBA, G8016

ABOVE RIGHT This is how the Golden Boy actually looks. STEPHANIE COWARD-YASKIW/LIFEIMAGESBYSTEPH

Despite its value and downtown prominence—bordered by Memorial Boulevard, Vaughan Street, and York and St. Mary avenues—it is generally overlooked by the public it is designed to serve.

Maybe it's overshadowed by the legislative building, which commands the view along the Memorial promenade. Perhaps it blends into other Tyndall Stone-clad government buildings nearby—the law courts, old Vaughan jail, and central powerhouse.

Whatever the reason, the archives building seems as tucked away as the materials it protects. Metal filing cabinets stand shoulder-to-shoulder, drawers deep and groaning with the weight of photographs, microfilm, audio cassettes, and documents. Temperature and humidity-controlled vaults store negatives, paintings, letters, journals, prints, and engravings. There are architectural plans and correspondence that give insight

FAR LEFT Original proposed designs for the Richardson Building at Portage and Main in Winnipeg, 1929, by Arthur A. Stoughton PROVINCIAL ARCHIVES OF MANITOBA, N7058

NEAR LEFT This is what the Richardson building actually looks like. DARREN BERNHARDT

Proposal for a new Winnipeg City Hall, 1912. PROVINCIAL ARCHIVES OF MANITOBA

into how things developed, and how different some things might have been, such as variations on the designs for the Golden Boy atop the legislative building (original plans show winged feet and a winged helmet, akin to the Greek god Hermes or Roman god Mercury) and the Richardson Building at Portage and Main (original plans are for an art deco design with a large clock). There is the winning design from a 1913 competition to replace Winnipeg's city hall. The plan was for a six-storey building in classical Greek Ionic style with multiple columns and a soaring clock tower. It was put on hold by a severe global recession, then shelved indefinitely by the First World War.

Past eras can be glimpsed through photographs that show mud paths where multi-lane roads now exist, tents and shacks where there are now

Firsts in the Northwest 1927-1938

1927

June 1: A crowd gathers at the town dock in Lac du Bonnet to watch a floatplane idle into the Winnipeg River then pull off into the sky, marking the first airmail service in Manitoba's history.

Many might not even know it is a special occasion and likely gathered at the site off Park Avenue to simply watch an airplane. Western Canada Airways Ltd. had established the province's first commercial airbase there earlier that spring.

That June 1 flight is just a test, but one with significant implications. With destinations to Bissett, Wadhope, and Slate Lake in Nopiming Provincial Park, the plane carries mail to see if such a service of delivery would be feasible. Lac du Bonnet is perfectly situated, with proximity to Winnipeg while offering an ideal location for seaplane service to isolated mining areas in central Manitoba.

The test convinces the Canada Post Office Department that the mail service will work, and it authorizes the country's first airmail service to begin later that year.

The pilot of the June flight, Capt. Frederick Joseph Stevenson, will go down as one of the country's most famous pioneering pilots. Many of his flights are made under primitive conditions, often with no landing fields, no lighting, no navigation or radio aids, and no facilities in which to do repairs—of which many are needed as the aircraft are not built to operate in extreme cold and frequently break down. Moreover, he sits in an open cockpit. But he is an innovative thinker, able to adjust to his challenges and conditions—even tying toboggans to the wheels of his craft to land on snow.

Capt. F.J. Stevenson PROVINCIAL ARCHIVES OF MANITOBA

On January 5, 1928, during a test flight in The Pas, Stevenson's engine fails, his plane goes into a spin at a low altitude and crashes onto a residential street, killing him on impact. His death marks another first for the country—the first pilot to be

high-rises. Documents chronicle natural devastation, turbulent political times, struggles by those who first settled the area and of those pushed out of it. There are celebrations of growth and achievement of a community that drew worldwide attention as it found its identity.

The building also fittingly houses the Hudson's Bay Company archives: 120-tons worth, including business transactions, medical records, personal journals of officials, inventories, and company reports dating from the company's founding in 1670.

Winnipeg has an ingrained connection to the company, which essentially founded the city. The HBC built Upper Fort Garry in 1822 near the confluence of the Red and Assiniboine Rivers. A fur-trading hub, the fort also served as administrative centre for the Red River Colony, established by HBC part-owner Thomas Douglas, better known as Lord Selkirk. That colony evolved into Winnipeg.

Later, as the company shifted from fur trading to retail, the HBC opened its first department store in Winnipeg in 1881, at the corner of Main Street and York Avenue. It closed when a new six-storey, 655,000-square-foot store opened in November 1926 at the corner of Portage Avenue and Memorial. It was the HBC's flagship store in western Canada. A street-level parking lot and service station was built at the south side of the building. In 1954, they were replaced by a multi-level parking structure—the first parkade on the Canadian prairies.

In 1970, on the 300th birthday of the company, the HBC's head office moved from England to Winnipeg, along with its archival collection. The head office later relocated to Toronto, but the collection remained behind, on loan to the Archives of Manitoba.

The records were permanently donated to the province in 1994 and include rare books from various trading posts and a portion of the personal library of fur trader Peter Fidler (1769-1822). The reading and research room of the Archives is also home to a working grandfather clock from 1684, its chimes tolling on the hour. Encased in walnut and trimmed in brass, the clock was built by John Ebsworth, an eminent clockmaker in England

who was appointed Master of the Clockmakers' Company in 1697.

The HBC was established under a royal charter by King Charles I in 1631, just as the craft of horology—watch and clockmaking—was starting to flourish in London. The 8.5-foot-tall clock was originally purchased by the company for 15 British pounds (about $26 CDN). It originally stood in Scrivener's Hall, the HBC's first permanent office in London. From there it was moved six times before winding up in Winnipeg in 1974, as part of the transfer of the HBC archives.

Grandfather clock from 1684 in the reading and research room of the Manitoba Provincial Archives DARREN BERNHARDT

The clock and wealth of archival materials is all free for the public to explore. Yet the hallways and reading rooms are routinely quiet as a catacomb. It's a radical change from when the building was a frequent

Winnipeg Tribune circulation manager Sam Sigesmund delivers bundles of newspapers to pilot Fred Stevenson, to be flown to logging and mining camps in Manitoba's north in 1927. UNIVERSITY OF MANITOBA ARCHIVES & SPECIAL COLLECTIONS/*WINNIPEG TRIBUNE* PHOTO COLLECTION

Fred Stevenson's parents unveil the dedication plaque at Stevenson Field in 1932. UNIVERSITY OF MANITOBA ARCHIVES & SPECIAL COLLECTIONS/*WINNIPEG TRIBUNE* PHOTO COLLECTION

killed in a commercial flying accident in Canada.

Four months later, an airfield in the Rural Municipality of St. James, outside of Winnipeg, opens and is named Stevenson Aerodrome in his honour. It consists of a tiny cabin, a twelve-foot hangar for storing folding-wing aircraft, and sod and clay runways on 165 acres of prairie land.

In the nearby Brookside Cemetery, Stevenson's final resting place faces southwest, toward the airfield that bears his name.

The airfield is now the site of Winnipeg's international airport, and it bears the name of another pioneer: James Armstrong Richardson, the man who owned Western Canada Airways and hired Stevenson to fly that inaugural test flight.

1930

After being first to install signal boxes in North America, the Winnipeg police service jumps back into the forefront of communications technology with the introduction of the first radio-equipped patrol cars in Canada.

Radio is a big improvement as it is wireless; however, it is still limited to one-way broadcasts. Messages are sent from the precinct to the car,

destination for crowds as a hub of high culture and popular entertainment.

In its past life, as the Winnipeg Auditorium, the building housed the Winnipeg Art Gallery, the Manitoba Museum, a roller rink, a wrestling and boxing arena, a concert hall, and a convention centre, and hosted live theatre.

Winnipeg Civic Auditorium under construction in 1932 PROVINCIAL ARCHIVES OF MANITOBA

RELIEF PROJECT

The first people to benefit from the $1.2-million facility were those down-and-out during the Great Depression. The building was an unemployment relief project funded jointly by the city, provincial, and federal governments.

Construction, which began in 1931, was spread among several companies and tradespeople to boost local economic benefits as much as possible. Workers had to be residents of Winnipeg for at least a year and be married or single with dependents. Aside from the engineers and foremen, 85 per cent of the crew were unemployed men registered for relief.

Working mostly by hand, hauling mud by truck and horse cart, they installed 127 support pillars, which reached down as far as 60 feet below sidewalk level to bedrock. The hulking caissons measured 3.5 feet to 5.5 feet in diameter and were set up strategically based on estimated load points.

"Nothing short of a disastrous earthquake can shake the Winnipeg Auditorium from its

Poster celebrating the opening day of the Winnipeg Civic Auditorium *WINNIPEG FREE PRESS SPECIAL SECTION, OCT. 15, 1932*

solid foundations," the *Winnipeg Evening Tribune* reported in October 1932 as the finishing work was being done, just before the building welcomed the public.

The roles it filled are now served by five separate buildings around the city: the Winnipeg Art Gallery, the Manitoba Museum, the Centennial Concert Hall, the Winnipeg Convention Centre, and the Canada Life Centre. It was a design marvel for the time with a large auditorium on one side, a concert hall on the other, and a shared backstage area between them.

The auditorium sat 4,135 and had its main entrance on St. Mary Avenue, facing the now-former HBC building (it closed in 2020). The entryway steps stretched across the face of the building, allowing large crowds to enter and

The roles it filled are now served by five separate buildings around the city.

exit with ease. Carved into the exterior stone just below the roofline were the words "Winnipeg Auditorium". These words were later hidden by renovations when the building's purpose shifted.

Through the St. Mary doors, visitors walked into a long lobby with ticket booths and coat-check rooms, then into a two-storey-high foyer. Wide staircases winged out at either end, leading to balcony seating in the auditorium or to the

Civic Auditorium ticket counter, 1930s PROVINCIAL ARCHIVES OF MANITOBA

but the only way officers can respond is to use a street corner signal box. There is no expectation, in most instances, for an officer to answer. Rather, they typically go directly to the address in the dispatch.

The radios are also operated by batteries and can only be used twelve hours at a time. They must be recharged the rest of the time. And the batteries are unwieldy, contained in a large box that takes up an entire portion of the back seat.

Still, they prove valuable in July 1934 when Sgt. John Verne of the St. Boniface police force is shot.

He responds at 8:15 a.m. to a robbery at a pharmacy on St. Mary's Road near Horace Street. Moments before he arrives, the robber carjacks a passing vehicle and forces the driver to go to the Union Station train depot on Main Street.

Verne gives chase and the vehicles race behind the station into the train yards. Verne gets ahead and forces the commandeered vehicle to stop. He and the robber get out, and before Verne can react, his stomach takes two bullets from a Colt .455 revolver.

The robber speeds away again in the car while two witnesses to the robbery, who also followed the pursuit, rush Verne to hospital. Another finds a beat cop and gives the licence plate number of the getaway car. The officer calls it in at a signal box and the message is broadcast to every radio-equipped patrol car, one which is on Main at Bannatyne Avenue as the wanted car passes.

The killer is captured at 8:50 a.m. but 39-year-old Verne dies. His killer is hanged in the gallows in February 1935, at age 34. As per a macabre custom of the time, a mugshot of the killer, framed by part of the rope that hung him, is given to the St. Boniface police department.

1931
February 2: Stevenson Aerodrome in the Rural Municipality of St. James, just west of Winnipeg, becomes Canada's first international airport when Northwest Airways launches a passenger and mail service between Winnipeg and Pembina, North Dakota.

By 1935, Northwest is running a daily service between Winnipeg and Chicago, with stops between at Pembina, Grand Forks, Fargo, Minneapolis, and Milwaukee.

Summer: Western Canada's first rooftop garden opens at a cost of about $100,000.

lower-level exhibition area. Glass display cabinets lined the east and west corridors of the auditorium foyer, creating an exhibition gallery for advertisers and manufacturers to showcase their products.

Other doors from the foyer led to the floor seating of the auditorium. All chairs in the venue were leather upholstered. The floor seats could be removed to clear space for sporting events and dances or for a raised platform to expand

Civic Auditorium exhibition galleries, 1930s PROVINCIAL ARCHIVES OF MANITOBA N23113

First recital at the Civic Auditorium, Nov. 9, 1932 P.M. ADAM, WINNIPEG IN FOCUS: CITY OF WINNIPEG ARCHIVES

the stage to accommodate large choirs or fashion show runways.

At the south end of the building, off York Avenue, was the entrance and lobby to the concert hall, which sat 800 people. The street-level door led to a modest foyer with stairs at each side that led to the lower exhibition level. There were no balconies in that hall, which was used for more intimate events like recitals, lectures, and live theatre.

The building also had four other smaller entryways from the street—two sets off Vaughan Street and two off Memorial Boulevard.

The shared stage area between the auditorium and concert hall was 56 feet wide and 34 feet deep and linked to a soundproof control room for radio broadcasting. The curtain opening was 40 feet wide for the auditorium and 30 feet for the concert hall. The ceiling in the stage area could be adjusted to direct acoustics to whichever side needed it.

One exhibition hall on the lower level showcased automobiles or farm equipment at various times of the year. Vehicle access was through ramps off York Avenue. The other hall welcomed a different set of wheels as home to a roller rink that had skaters circle the building's thick support posts.

Car show in the lower level of Civic Auditorium, 1940s WINNIPEG IN FOCUS: CITY OF WINNIPEG ARCHIVES

A sign for roller skating hangs outside the Civic Auditorium doors facing Memorial Boulevard at St. Mary Avenue, 1952. PROVINCIAL ARCHIVES OF MANITOBA, N4362

The second floor, or mezzanine level, contained the upper level of the exhibition galleries for advertisers and manufacturers, along with smaller committee rooms, the first row of balconies in the auditorium, and gender-divided lounges.

An assembly hall with seating for 400, used for conventions and other meetings, was located on the third floor, along with the art gallery and museum. The assembly hall was above the St. Mary entrance, while the museum filled the east side of the building, and the art gallery took up the west—with a sightline across the street to where the current art gallery stands.

The 65-by-123-foot greenspace is on top of a three-storey brick apartment building at 508 Sherbrook Street in Winnipeg.

1932
May 26: The Canadian Radio Broadcasting Commission (CRBC), Canada's first public broadcaster—precursor to the Canadian Broadcasting Corporation—is created. It comes from the lobbying efforts of Graham Spry, former editor of the University of Manitoba's student newspaper.

While still a student, Spry becomes an editorial writer for the *Manitoba Free Press* and is mentored by editor John W. Dafoe, a passionate Canadian nationalist. When Spry goes overseas to study at Oxford University as a Rhodes Scholar, Dafoe's zeal remains with him.

Once he returns to Canada, he becomes involved with the Canadian Clubs, which encourage interest in public affairs. Spry organizes a nationwide radio broadcast in 1917 to celebrate the fiftieth anniversary of Confederation. He pulls it off despite a lack of a national radio network.

The accomplishment, along with the growing use of airwaves in following years to deride the government, prompt Ottawa to launch a royal commission to examine radio broadcasting abroad and how it can be better adopted in Canada.

The Aird Commission's report is released in 1929 and recommends the creation of a publicly funded national broadcaster. An election and change of government leaves the report sitting on a shelf. Spry establishes the Canadian Radio League in 1930 to mobilize support for public broadcasting in Canada.

As a result of the lobbying efforts, the CRBC is established in 1932 by Prime Minister R.B. Bennett. And on November 2, 1936, the CRBC is re-established as a Crown corporation, becoming the CBC.

July 1: The first western link between two provinces is officially opened between Manitoba and Ontario. The Winnipeg-Kenora highway, about 235 kilometres in length, was built by workers employed by government relief programs during the Great Depression. The route opens to vehicles on June 2, but the ceremony and ribbon cutting is held on Dominion Day, July 1.

It took more than a decade before the Winnipeg-Kenora link became part of the

The third floor also had a number of office spaces, the upper part of the concert hall, the remaining balcony seats for the auditorium, and another set of gender-specific lounges.

Another fourteen rooms, ranging in size from 25-75 seats, were located throughout the remainder of the building. Connecting everything was the building's own telephone exchange, with extra cables for press and telegraph services. The sheer size of the building and all that it offered earned it the unofficial title of convention centre of Canada.

The Canadian Broadcasting Corporation had some studios in the basement for a brief time in

The sheer size of the building and all that it offered earned it the unofficial title of convention centre of Canada.

the 1960s, and the City of Winnipeg's Parks and Recreation Department ran programs from the basement as well. That's where, in 1948, Charles Barbour began to reinvent the city's lagging and underfunded recreation services and community centres. After securing more money, he introduced a six-man football league and played a key role in bringing Little League Baseball to the city. Not only did Barbour increase the number of activities in the city system, but he also diversified them. He created programs for handicrafts, hobbies, music, art, and drama to appeal to all ages, sexes, and abilities. Under Barbour's direction, the city's first recreational programming for adults was launched, with an emphasis on seniors.

ART GALLERY OPENING

Winnipeg's first art gallery opened in the Manitoba Hotel, at Main Street and Water Avenue (now William Stephenson Way) in the mid-1890s but its time there was short. The hotel burned to rubble in 1899.

7,821-kilometre Trans-Canada Highway, which was eventually built between 1949 and 1970.

1936
Born in Wakaw, Saskatchewan, in 1911, Mary Annie Wawrykow moves to Winnipeg where she attends the University of Manitoba Law School and is called to the Manitoba Bar in 1936, becoming the first female lawyer of Ukrainian descent in Canada.

She is made a Queen's Counsel in 1965 in recognition of her exceptional ability in Manitoba's legal profession. Three years later she is appointed judge of the Winnipeg Juvenile and Family Court, and in 1975 she becomes responsible for the Provincial Judges' Court of Winnipeg (North).

1938
Winnipeg's Elinor Frances Elizabeth Black, a Kelvin High School graduate, becomes the first

Dr. Elinor F. E. Black
UNIVERSITY OF MANITOBA COLLEGE OF MEDICINE ARCHIVES

Canadian woman member of the British Royal College of Obstetricians and Gynaecologists. In 1961, she is elected the first female president of the Society of Obstetricians and Gynaecologists of Canada.

Elizabeth Dundas Long, a former reporter for the *Winnipeg Tribune* and then editor with *the Manitoba Free Press*, joins CBC as head of women's programs for all of Canada. That makes her the first woman hired in an executive capacity at the national public broadcaster, a position she held until she retired in 1956.

December 20: Canada's first helicopter is designed, built, and flown by three brothers in a small southeastern Manitoba community called Homewood.

The Froebe flyer is the creation of Nicholas, Douglas, and Theodore Froebe, who are backyard tinkerers with mechanically gifted minds. Between them, they share skills in design, mechanics, and welding.

The aircraft-grade metal tubing for the frame is bought in Winnipeg, and some other materials, including the engine, are bought at a used aircraft dealership in the US. But

Doug Froebe sits in the original Froebe helicopter for a test run in the fall of 1938. ROYAL AVIATION MUSEUM OF WESTERN CANADA

many other parts are handcrafted or salvaged from automotive and farm machinery around the brothers' property.

The helicopter is thirteen feet, seven inches long with two wheels at the front and one at back. The pilot sits in a single seat at the rear of the frame, with the engine in front.

The first flight, piloted by Doug, gets about three feet off the ground. It moves a short distance and hovers

From the ruins in 1911 rose the Industrial Bureau Exposition Building (also called the Board of Trade building), with the Winnipeg Museum of Fine Arts opening there in 1912 as the first admission-free venue of its kind in North America. The Winnipeg School of Arts opened there the following year. In 1923, the two united to become the Winnipeg Gallery and School of Arts.

Financial issues led to the gallery suspending operations by 1926, with its collection held in trust by the school of art. The gallery resumed operations in April 1932 when it reopened in the Civic Auditorium. The school of art stayed at the Board of Trade building until that facility was demolished in 1935. The school relocated twice before it split off from the gallery and became part of the University of Manitoba and its campus.

The gallery remained part of the Civic Auditorium until September 1971 when it moved into its own purpose-built building—and where it remains today—across the street and one block down from the auditorium at the Winnipeg Art Gallery. It later added art classes and then

Museum display cases inside the Civic Auditorium, 1933
PROVINCIAL ARCHIVES OF MANITOBA N15756

expanded in 2021 to include Qaumajuq, a museum for the largest public collection of contemporary Inuit art in the world.

PACKED TO THE ROOF

From the day the doors opened for the first concert, which drew 3,300 people, the building was a magnet for the masses. During its heyday, the auditorium packed in crowds for a wide variety of events.

U of Manitoba convocation ceremony at Civic Auditorium PROVINCIAL ARCHIVES OF MANITOBA

Louis Armstrong, "Trumpet King of Swing", plays with his band at the Civic Auditorium in June 1942. WINNIPEG IN FOCUS: CITY OF WINNIPEG ARCHIVES

In January 1946 it hosted a welcome back celebration for the Winnipeg Grenadiers, an infantry regiment of the Canadian Army returning from the Second World War battlefronts.

Prime Minister John Diefenbaker opened his election campaign there on February 12, 1958, and so many people turned out that both the auditorium and concert hall were filled.

A few months later the Canadian Labour Congress and CCF (Co-operative Commonwealth Federation) met in the auditorium to lay plans for the creation of the New Democratic Party.

In 1968, some sixty bishops and archbishops read mass in four languages—English, French, Latin and Greek—to 3,200 people attending the Catholic Conference.

The main auditorium was also home to the Winnipeg Symphony Orchestra, the Winnipeg Philharmonic Choir, the evening sessions of the Manitoba (Winnipeg) Music Competition Festival, and the Gee Celebrity Concerts. International musicians that performed in the building over the years includes Johnny

Cash, The Byrds, Duke Ellington, Glenn Gould, Sergei Rachmaninoff, various opera companies, ballets, and The Trapp Family Singers, whose lives were fictionalized in 1959—fourteen years after their Winnipeg show—in *The Sound of Music*. The last concert was The Beach Boys on November 30, 1969.

MUSEUM OPENING

The Civic Auditorium became home in December 1932 to what would eventually become the largest museum in the province.

The Manitoba Museum, then called the Museum of Man and Nature, exhibited a collection of Indigenous arrowheads, flints and axes as well as moths and butterflies from around the world.

"The old museum was not large, but it was clearly a pleasant place to spend an afternoon examining cabinets of archaeological artefacts, First Nations clothing, stuffed birds, and fossils," Graham Young, the present museum's curator of geology and paleontology wrote in a blog, "The

for about twenty minutes. It is the first person-controlled vertical flight in Canada.

The brothers make adjustments, and the ensuing flights reach up to six feet off the ground with distances over fifty feet. By March 1939 they record a series of short flights for a total of four hours and five minutes of flight time.

But as the Depression era deepens, money is hard to come by. The brothers try unsuccessfully to sell their design to the US during the Second World War. The helicopter is put into storage in a granary on the family farm and forgotten until it is rediscovered in the 1970s.

Froebe brothers—Doug, Nicholas, and Theodore—on their farm in Homewood in the mid-1930s ROYAL AVIATION MUSEUM OF WESTERN CANADA

The machine, along with Doug's notebooks, logbook, and letters, is now in the Royal Aviation Museum of Western Canada in Winnipeg. A stone cairn honouring the pioneering flights now stands in Homewood, just east of Carman.

Old Museum Lives On," on January 31, 2013. "It was very much a 'cabinet of curiosities' of the old school, and a good one."

Over the years the collection grew, and the museum's limited space forced it to create small, makeshift galleries on other floors of the auditorium building. With storage full, the museum had to reluctantly turn away donations, including a Red River cart, according to a blog post by Heritage Winnipeg, "A Keystone of Culture: The Manitoba Museum."

"The museum's director, L.T.S. Norris-Elye, yearned to display a replica of the room that Louis Riel occupied at Upper Fort Garry, filled with valuable authentic artifacts. But even with free rent … [it] could not afford additional staff, never mind a new building," the blog stated.

Souvenir booklet for the Manitoba Museum when it was located inside the Civic Auditorium DARREN BERNHARDT

That changed with the approach of two milestone anniversaries—Canada's centennial in 1967 and Manitoba's in 1970—and a plan to commemorate them.

The Manitoba Centennial Arts Centre, a concept pitched by Premier Duff Roblin, was part legacy project and part urban renewal effort. Developed on thirty-four acres of land at the fringe of downtown and Exchange District, it is today's city hall complex, Centennial Concert Hall, Manitoba Museum, Planetarium and Science Gallery, and Royal Manitoba Theatre Centre.

Years earlier, Winnipeg Mayor Stephen Juba had been eyeing changes in the same area. He wanted out of the 1886 city hall. It was affectionately and nostalgically referred to as the gingerbread city hall for its ornate Victorian appearance, but it was also old and crumbling. Juba suggested demolishing it and offering the land for the Manitoba Museum to build a state-of-the-art facility. As for a new city hall, Juba's eyes were locked onto the civic auditorium.

He had an architect draw up a proposed redesign of that building, adding four additional storeys to accommodate all civic offices and the Winnipeg School Board. It would centralize the city's administration near the seat of the provincial government.

The estimated cost was $2.5 million but that was only for the redesign. The total cost of Juba's plan was $4.5 million, because it meant gutting the auditorium and building a new entertainment centre somewhere else.

By 1960, Juba gave up on his plan as Roblin's took hold, but the threat to the future of the auditorium had already put wheels in motion. Winnipeg Enterprises Corporation, which brought many entertainment and sports attractions to the city, opened its own 9,500 seat Winnipeg Arena in 1955 and shifted its business there.

SOLD TO THE PROVINCE

In 1970 the building was sold to the province for $1 million.

The city asked $1.3 million, but the province offered $750,000 before the two sides settled in the middle.

The sale surprised the building's manager, who told the media he was led to believe it was going to be invested in, not dumped by the city. He abruptly resigned, followed by a member of the commission who was in charge of the facility's operation.

The change was also lamented in the press: "The walls, which echoed for almost half a century to some of the sweetest live sound in the world, will house government offices and serve as a tomb for the provincial archives," stated an article in *The Winnipeg Free Press* in April 1970.

"Well, the curtain has fallen on all of this now," a *Tribune* article stated. "The shift of the cultural scene to Main Street and the sale of the Winnipeg Auditorium, mark the end of an entertainment era…Whatever its function in the future, the shell of that auditorium building will stand a reminder of incredible times [and] incredible audiences."

Manitoba Archives storage section in the old Winnipeg Art Gallery area, November 2023 DARREN BERNHARDT

"The walls, which echoed for almost half a century to some of the sweetest live sound in the world, will house government offices and serve as a tomb for the provincial archives." *The Winnipeg Free Press*

The building underwent extensive renovations in the early 1970s to the tune of $4 million. The main auditorium balconies were removed, creating a vast open space fifty feet high. That became vault space, as well as stacks for the legislative library's collection. The former museum and art exhibition galleries, with their large arched windows, are now the public reading and research rooms.

The main entrance off St. Mary no longer exists. It's now encased by windows and covered by a patinated copper roof. The area that was the main foyer is now offices for Elections Manitoba and the grand staircase that led up to that entrance has been levelled off by concrete slabs and blocked from the public sidewalk by a concrete wall.

Offices, storerooms, and staff areas occupy the central section of what used to be the auditorium. The concert hall survived the 1970s reno but by the early 1980s it was no longer in use. It was then boxed off and transformed into the HBC vaults.

At the 1975 reopening of the building as the Archives of Manitoba and Legislative Library of Manitoba, Public Works Minister Russ Doern used a 1777 sword to slice through a scarlet ribbon. Newspaper articles expressed how unrecognizable the building was from its former identity. But there were fragments of its former self, and more than fifty years since, some are still there—if you look closely.

The maze of hallways meanders alongside and behind a sloped floor, which was the old riser for seats in the concert hall. And in the basement, some of the pillars still display flaking and faded paint from the roller rink days.

Reading and research area in the Manitoba Archives, in an area that was once part of an exhibition gallery. DARREN BERNHARDT

Painted support posts from the Civic Auditorium's roller rink days are seen in November 2023. The area is now used for storage. DARREN BERNHARDT

PUNKINHEAD
MANITOBA-MADE
RIVAL TO RUDOLPH

Rudolph has ruled Christmas since 1939 as the most beloved sidekick, but there was a time that a mop-topped bear born in Winnipeg gave the red-nosed reindeer a run for the title.

Punkinhead was dreamt up on a drawing board in a rooming house in Winnipeg's West End and became the most successful advertising character in Canadian retail history.

It all started in 1947 when executives at Eaton's department store headquarters in Toronto, Ontario decided to flat-out copy the hugely successful game plan of the US-based retailer Montgomery Ward—but to wrap it up differently.

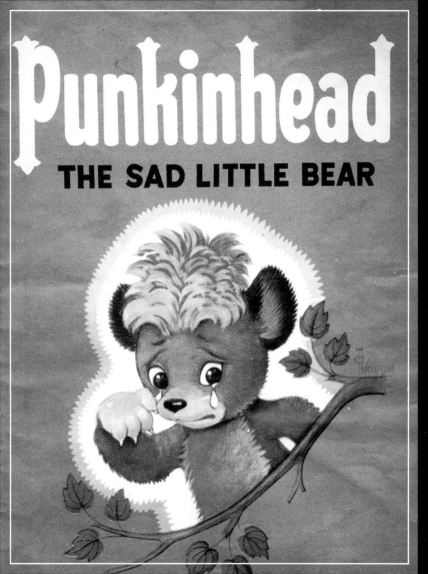

Punkinhead debuted in the 1948 story, *The Sad Little Bear.* CANADIAN ANIMATION, CARTOONING AND ILLUSTRATION/CANADIANACI.CA

Eaton's
Mail Order
Christmas
Book, 1954-55
ARCHIVES OF
ONTARIO/T. EATON
CO. FONDS

A letter to kids
from Santa
Claus and
Punkinhead,
circa 1950s. It
was issued in
response to
letters kids sent
to Saint Nick
through Eaton's.
ARCHIVES OF
ONTARIO/T. EATON
CO. FONDS

Coke is responsible for the image North Americans associate with old Saint Nick. The jolly, portly grandfatherly figure in a white beard, red outfit cuffed in white fur, black boots and black belt, and carrying a sack of toys first appeared in 1931. The character was drawn up by illustrator Haddon Sundblom, commissioned to design the character for Coca-Cola's Christmas adverts.

Montgomery Ward latched onto Santa's popularity by devising Rudolph eight years later as a Christmas helper with a hard-luck backstory. He was introduced to the world through colouring books given out each Christmas to attract shoppers to its stores. The flying misfit reindeer became a wildly successful marketing mascot—the same way Santa Claus was for the Coca-Cola corporation. And just eight years after that, Eaton's did the same thing, substituting the reindeer with a teddy bear named Punkinhead.

Both Rudolph and Punkinhead sported a physical trait that made them targets of ridicule from their so-called friends, causing them to be ostracized. But it was that uniqueness, in both

Punkinhead lived in Bear Land where his unwieldy, ginger-blond tuft of fuzz made him stand out from the other bears.

cases, that helped save Santa in his greatest time of need. Rudolph's glowing honker lit a path through the foggy night so Santa could fly his sleigh and deliver presents. For Punkinhead, his tangle of hair enabled a party hat to fit just right and save a parade.

Page from Punkinhead's 1948 debut book, *The Sad Little Bear* CANADIAN ANIMATION, CARTOONING AND ILLUSTRATION/ CANADIANACI.CA

Punkinhead lived in Bear Land where his unwieldy, ginger-blond tuft of fuzz made him stand out from the other bears and their velvety smooth heads. Feeling rejected, the jilted bear went off to be alone.

One of Santa's clown's falls ill from overindulging on honey sodas in Punkinhead's 1948 debut book.

Just before Christmas, Santa and his crew of fairies, gnomes, clowns, and elves were on their way from the North Pole to Toyland to put on a big parade. They made a pit stop for honey soda drinks in Bear Land where one of the clowns overindulged and was stricken with a rip-roaring bellyache. Santa turned to the bears for a last-minute replacement. Many tried to fill the role but couldn't complete the clown costume because the hat kept sliding off their sleek domes.

Santa was about to give up when the bears remembered Punkinhead and ran off to get him. When Punkinhead tried on the hat, his woolly hair kept it in place. He became an important part of the parade and Santa's favourite little helper. Take that, Rudolph.

Eaton's executives handed the story idea to Winnipeg illustrator Charles Thorson to make it come alive. The company already had a long history with Thorson, who was chief illustrator of the Eaton's catalogue from 1914 to 1935, a time when all images were hand-drawn.

Born in Gimli in 1890 to Icelandic parents, Thorson started his path in illustration as a polit-ical cartoonist for two newspapers that served the Icelandic commun-ity north of Winnipeg.

Charlie Thorson portrait
UNIVERSITY OF MANITOBA
ARCHIVES AND SPECIAL
COLLECTIONS/
CHARLIE THORSON FONDS

He also designed the uniform and crest for the Winnipeg Falcons, a team composed mostly of Icelandic men unable to join other teams due to ethnic prejudices who cobbled together their own squad in 1911 and named themselves after Iceland's national bird. The Falcons became a dynamo that went on to represent Canada in the 1920 Olympic games in Antwerp, Belgium. They won all their games by a combined score of

Firsts in the Northwest 1940-1956

1940

The paint roller is invented by Norman Breakey, a Manitoban living in Toronto.

Next to the safety pin, it is considered the most widely used invention on the planet. But Breakey does not make any money from his invention. He dies a poor man.

Born in 1891 in Pierson, a small rural community in southwest Manitoba, he works in a hardware store in Souris. After the war, he resettles in Toronto and returns to the hard-ware business, operating a store in the Leaside neighbourhood.

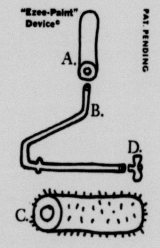

Norman Breakey paint roller
BRANDON SUN, APRIL 19, 1975

He invents a device he calls The Little Red Devil, which uses hydraulic pressure to tap beer kegs stored in the basement of a pub and sends the liquid to the first-floor bar. It is never patented but is used by several pubs.

Soon after, he comes up with the roller idea, perhaps from being around paint supplies all day.

He starts production on his own and sells a

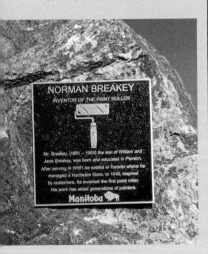

Norman Breakey monument in Pierson, Manitoba THE DUBIOUS HAUSFRAU, ATLAS OBSCURA

few rollers locally, wrapping them in fabric used to cover passenger train seats. The original roller trays are hammered out by a tinsmith. He markets them as the Koton Kotor and sells some to Eaton's, which renames them as the Teco (T. Eaton Co.) roller.

Despite some small success, Breakey has trouble finding financial backers to manufacture and distribute the roller on a wider scale.

Meanwhile, other entrepreneurs begin to create their own versions. One of those is Richard Croxton Adams, who works for the Sherwin-Williams paint company in Cleveland, Ohio. He claims his idea

is prompted by a shortage of paint brushes due to the Second World War's impact on production. His roller has a slight adjustment to Breakey's and gets patented in 1942.

It is not clear if Breakey applies for a patent or not, or if he never got beyond the pending stage to complete it. Some articles say he didn't have the money to pay for the patent, while others say he just forgot to do it. Another says Breakey was given an opportunity to defend his patent and prove it was his design, but he didn't have the finances to challenge Adams, who found investors and tapped into the much larger

American market, becoming a wealthy man.

Breakey dies in 1965. A monument and plaque honouring him and his invention stands in Pierson.

1941

Mary Margaret "Margery" Brooker, a former teacher at Cecil Rhodes School in Winnipeg, is appointed as a school inspector for the Virden District by the Manitoba Department of Education. She becomes the first woman in Canada to be appointed to such a position and works in that role for fourteen years, inspecting rural schools. In 1948 she is appointed school inspector in the Winnipeg School District.

29-1 and brought home Canada's first Olympic gold medal in ice hockey.

Thorson moved to California in 1935 to try his hand at the emerging craft of animation. He was hired on the spot by Walt Disney. Thorson designed some of Disney's best-known characters, including Snow White and the dwarves. He created six dwarves—which was the original plan—then Disney added a seventh, Dopey, as a late addition from another animator.

Thorson claimed Snow White was based on a Winnipeg waitress, Kristin Solvadottir, who worked at the Wevel Cafe near the corner of Sargent Avenue and Victor Street in the city's West End.

Snow White and the Seven Dwarfs became Disney's first fully animated feature film and is the only film to have been honoured by the Academy of Motion Picture Arts and Sciences in two successive years. In 1937, the year of its release, it was nominated for best music (scoring) but

Thorson claimed Snow White was based on a Winnipeg waitress, Kristin Solvadottir, who worked at the Wevel Cafe near the corner of Sargent Avenue and Victor Street in the city's West End.

Kristin Solvadottir

didn't win. In 1938, the Academy honoured *Snow White* as "a significant screen innovation which has charmed millions and pioneered a great new entertainment field for the motion picture cartoon." Disney was presented with a special award consisting, appropriately, of one full-size Oscar and seven miniature statuettes.

Despite his contributions, which included working on the film's storyline, Thorson's name was not on the credits. It was Walt Disney's policy to impose anonymity on his workers, and that didn't sit well with Thorson. He left in anger and was hired by Warner Bros. to conceive characters they hoped would challenge Disney's reign in animated entertainment. His new bosses asked Thorson to design a rabbit for a cartoon, *Hare-um Scare-um*, to be made by director Cal Dalton and animator Ben "Bugs" Hardaway. Thorson labelled his model sheet as "Bug's Bunny" and the name stuck, according to Gene Walz's book, *Cartoon Charlie: The Life and Art of Animation Pioneer Charles Thorson.*

Drawing from 1939 of Charlie Thorson's Bugs Bunny, created for Merry Melodies Studios UNIVERSITY OF MANITOBA ARCHIVES AND SPECIAL COLLECTIONS/CHARLIE THORSON FONDS

Hare-um Scare-um is the first appearance of the rabbit as the grey, large-footed hare he would fully evolve into through redesigns by other animators in successive years. In 1940, after some tweaks by designer Tex Avery, Bugs looked more like his present-day character.

That same year Bugs met Elmer Fudd, who would become his chief antagonist in place of Porky, launching one of the most famous rivalries in cinema history. Elmer was also Thorson's design, based on a prototype by Avery. Bugs and Elmer were two of the biggest stars of the so-called golden age of American animation (1928-1960) and continue to endure as two of the world's most popular cartoon characters.

1946

Fred Wilmot joins the *Winnipeg Citizen* newspaper as Canada's first Black full-time daily reporter.

Born in Toronto in 1918 to Jamaican parents who move to that city in 1911, Wilmot is introduced to racism at an early age. His dad is an electrical contractor who is denied entry to the electricians' union because he is Black.

When the Second World War breaks out, Wilmot tries to join the Canadian military with other boys from his street but is told it is a white man's war. He ultimately serves as a "zombie"—a soldier who stays on the home

Fred Wilmot in February 1945, from the pages of *Wallace Shipbuilder*, the Burrard Dry Dock Company's employee newsletter. MUSEUM AND ARCHIVES OF NORTH VANCOUVER

front in Canada—doing various jobs.

He later reports to the National Resources Mobilization Board and is assigned to a rivet gang in the Vancouver shipyards. After some time, Wilmot

starts writing a column for *The Main Deck*, the union newspaper, then for the *Pacific Advocate*, a weekly newspaper for the British Columbia section of the Canadian Communist Party.

Not one to stay put for too long, Wilmot becomes a freelance writer and broadcaster for the CBC before he joins the *Winnipeg Citizen* in 1946.

At some point, he leaves the paper to become publicity director for the Manitoba Red Cross and then secretary of the Winnipeg Labour Committee Against Racial Intolerance, an organization formed by the city's three major labour councils.

It carries out educational campaigns denouncing discrimination, with Wilmot emphasizing the need for a concerted campaign for racial friendship.

1949

Harlequin Enterprises, the world's largest publisher of romance fiction, is founded in Winnipeg by Richard Henry Gardyn Bonnycastle.

Born in Binscarth, Manitoba, he attends England's Oxford University and is a member of the ice hockey team that includes future Prime Minister of Canada Lester B. Pearson and future Governor General of Canada Roland Michener.

At age 22 in 1925, Bonnycastle ditches a fledgling law career to become a fur trader for the Hudson's Bay Company. For eleven years, he lives in the western Arctic and becomes chief fur trader, later publishing his adventure diaries in 1984.

He moves back to Winnipeg in 1937 and works as an HBC senior manager until 1945, when he shifts careers to become managing director for Advocate Printers, a branch of Toronto's Bryant Press. While there, Bonnycastle shepherds the creation of Harlequin to reprint low-cost mass-market books in paperback, primarily to keep the presses busy. Initially, it's a partnership between Advocate, Doug Weld of Bryant Press, and Jack Palmer, Canadian distributor for the *Saturday Evening Post* and *Ladies' Home Journal*. Harlequin takes in a little of everything: mysteries, westerns, true crime, fiction, sports, cookbooks and romance.

As the company struggles in the 1950s, Bonnycastle secures 75 per cent ownership. Under his navigation, and guidance from his wife Mary Northwood, the company is set back on course.

Northwood is an avid reader of romance novels from British publisher Mills & Boon and believes a market exists for them in North America. In 1957, Harlequin strikes a deal to become the exclusive North American distributor. Most North American booksellers are reluctant to stock mass-market paperbacks, so Harlequin chooses to distribute them to supermarkets, drug stores, and other retail outlets.

Bonnycastle dies of a heart attack in 1968 and his son, Richard Jr., steps in, propelling Harlequin Enterprises even further. The headquarters move to Toronto in 1969, where the booming company purchases Mills & Boon in 1971.

No longer owned by the Bonnycastle family, Harlequin Enterprises is now a division of HarperCollins Canada. It produces a book every five seconds and translates them into 29 languages. It has sold more than 6.8 billion books since it started.

Since the 1990s Harlequin has also become a major producer of made-for-TV movies, many filmed in Winnipeg, where it all began.

Richard Henry Gardyn Bonnycastle is commemorated by R.H.G. Bonnycastle School in Waverley Heights and Bonnycastle

During his time south of the border, Thorson designed and developed characters at nearly every major Hollywood animation studio before shifting to smaller studios in Miami and then New York. Aside from Bugs, Elmer, and Snow White, his portfolio includes Sniffles the Mouse, Little Hiawatha, and redesigns of Popeye and the Raggedy Ann and Andy characters. He also created more than a hundred characters and creatures for an ill-fated animated TV series called *The Stone Age*. That cartoon would eventually become *The Flintstones*.

Unfortunately, just as prolific as his creative output were Thorson's temper and problematic drinking. They often got the better of him and led to his departures from several studios. He returned to Winnipeg in 1946 and settled into a rooming house in the West End. When Eaton's came calling in 1947, Thorson was freelancing and looking for work. The bear debuted in the 1948 story *Punkinhead: The Sad Little Bear*, just in time for his first appearance in Eaton's Santa Claus parade in Toronto—the largest Christmas

Park, tucked between Assiniboine Avenue and the Assiniboine River, between Main Street and the Midtown Bridge.

1950

The plastic garbage bag, later manufactured under the Glad brand, is invented by Harry Wasylyk.

Born in Narol, just northeast of Winnipeg, Wasylyk is a businessman who founds the company Prairie Canners Ltd., as well as Food Products Ltd., which he uses to introduce polyethylene to Canada.

The waterproof, stretchy material was invented in the 1930s but Wasylyk uses a process called extrusion to heat tiny resin pellets then pressurize them to make them more pliable. The resin is then blown into sheets and sealed to form a bag. The motivation for Wasylyk comes from hearing staff at the Winnipeg General Hospital talk about the difficulty of keeping their garbage cans sanitary.

He creates the Polyethylene Bag Manufacturing Company with his wife and son, brother Walter Wasylyk, and business partner Larry Hansen of Lindsay, Ontario. Hansen is making his own garbage bags to use around the Union Carbide plant where he works but likes what Wasylyk is doing and buys into the business.

The company develops several plastic packaging products, including the green garbage bag, which is sold for commercial uses—the general hospital is one of the first clients. Union Carbide buys the invention and starts manufacturing the Glad garbage bags for home use in the late 1960s.

Wasylyk's plastic bag is now listed as being among the best Canadian inventions, alongside insulin, the game of basketball, the telephone, the snowblower and Superman.

1956

The first fast-food restaurant in Canada opens for business on Portage Avenue in Winnipeg in 1956.

Roy Allen and Frank Wright's A&W drive-ins are already a familiar sight in the United States with carhops carrying trays of burgers and frosty mugs of root beer. They choose Winnipeg as their first foray into Canada, a decade before McDonald's brings its golden arches.

It remains in that spot, across from Greenacre Boulevard, until 2015, when a new location is built a block away at Sturgeon Road.

"Kids wore Punkinhead watches, toques, mittens. They ate out of Punkinhead bowls and drank from Punkinhead mugs."

Roy MacGregor, *Globe and Mail*

parade in North America. The bear with the messy hair and short pants became a mid-century phenomenon.

"To say Punkinhead took off is an understatement," journalist Roy MacGregor wrote in a 2007 *Globe and Mail* article. "There were Eaton's-sponsored radio programs featuring both Santa and his little bear friend. Kids wore Punkinhead watches, toques, mittens. They ate out of Punkinhead bowls and drank from Punkinhead mugs. There was Punkinhead furniture—rocking horses, chairs—and even an official Punkinhead song."

Bill Isbister, a prominent musician and songwriter in Toronto, wrote "The Punkinhead Song" based on the original story. The recording sold 10,000 copies in the week before Christmas 1951 and another 28,000 in the immediate three weeks after Christmas. It was later picked up by various artists and recorded for major labels, including a version by country and western legend Wilf Carter.

The bear also became a major feature of Eaton's other major Canadian parade in Winnipeg. Cheers for Punkinhead easily matched those for Santa and soon he was promoted from walking the route to sitting in the highest profile spot: in the sleigh alongside the big man.

His image was a ubiquitous part of Eaton's Christmas advertising for the next decade. It

Merrythought Punkinhead teddy bear, circa 1951
CHRISTIE'S AUCTION HOUSE/ CHRISTIES.COM, DEC. 2002

was branded on hats, baby bottle warmers, bibs, bedside lamps, pyjamas, balls, bath towels, snowsuits, sweaters, slippers and much more. A series of Punkinhead stories were published every year until 1959 and given to kids who visited Santa at Eaton's Toyland.

[Punkinhead's] image was a ubiquitous part of Eaton's Christmas advertising for the next decade.

And of course, there were teddy bears. The originals were made in England, specifically for Eaton's, of mohair, stuffed with fine wood shavings, and fitted with glass eyes, a tuft of shaggy hair and little shorts.

Unlike the enduring enchantment of Rudolph, who remains an indelible part of the Christmas

[Thorson] likely could have retired on Punkinhead royalties alone, had he retained the copyright. Unfortunately, he sold it to Eaton's for $1 in 1949.

Punkinhead lamp
COLLECTORS WEEKLY/
COLLECTORSWEEKLY.COM

season, Punkinhead's appeal eventually faded. The wall-to-wall branding trickled off, though he continued to appear in the Santa Claus parade until 1982, when Eaton's ended its association with the event. It had paid for the parades from their inception–1905 in Toronto and 1909 in Winnipeg—but could no longer afford to do so.

Punkinhead was briefly revived by Eaton's in 1992 as the struggling retailer reached into its nostalgia bag to find that old merchandising magic and win back its customer base. It didn't work; the hundred-and-thirty-year-old company declared bankruptcy just seven years later. Its assets were purchased by Sears, which ran a few stores under the Eaton's banner until 2002 when the brand vanished. Sears Canada then ceased operations in 2018.

As for Thorson, he never cashed in on his creation. He likely could have retired on Punkinhead royalties alone, had he retained the copyright. Unfortunately, he sold it to Eaton's for $1 in 1949, according to the University of Manitoba Archives and Special Collections, which contains much of his work.

The hot-headed Thorson had been involved in the illustrations and story ideas for just the first three Punkinhead booklets before his temper got the best of him, leading to an unceremonious parting of ways with Eaton's. He cut ties with the company and his creation. According to Walz, Thorson was drunk at a party in his honour at Winnipeg's Fort Garry Hotel. He got into an argument with an Eaton's executive, threw a punch and was promptly fired.

In 1952, down on his luck and looking for work, Thorson designed Elmer the Safety Elephant for the Toronto police department's traffic-safety program. He struggled to find animation work beyond that and eventually finished his career where it began—in Winnipeg doing advertising work.

Punkinhead dish set CANADIAN ANIMATION, CARTOONING AND ILLUSTRATION/CANADIANACI.CA

Punkinhead may be gone, but he remains popular in some circles. The original teddy bears from England, produced between 1948 and the mid-1950s by a company called Merrythought, have become collectors' items, selling for thousands of dollars.

HOW MANITOBANS AMPLIFIED ROCK 'N' ROLL

That distinctive gritty, reverberating distortion punching through The Guess Who's classic song "American Woman" is the signature of a Winnipeg radio repairman whose ingenuity rocked the world of music.

The guitar is the work of fellow Winnipegger Randy Bachman, but the timbre he manifested through his instrument is the artistry of Gar Gillies, whose language was acoustics.

Thomas Garnet Gillies was born in Winnipeg in February 1921 and later gave birth himself—to a robust rock 'n' roll resonance that became known as the Winnipeg sound.

Stack of modern reproductions of the Herzog amp
GARNETAMPS.COM

Rock-Ola wall box, 1953 MADE-IN-CHICAGO MUSEUM/
MADEINCHICAGOMUSEUM.COM

In his teens, Gillies fell in love with the big band ensembles led by Nat King Cole and Tommy Dorsey. He became a jazz trombonist and started the Gar Gillies Jump Band, a seven-piece band that later evolved into the thirteen-piece Gar Gillies Big Band.

Gar Gillies, 1971 COURTESY HANS SIPMA

After graduating high school, he balanced his time touring with his band and working in the radio repair department at Eaton's. The combination of those two pursuits allowed Gillies to become something of an electronics engineer.

As the band moved into larger venues, it struggled to make itself heard over the din of audience conversations. Gillies designed and built an amplifier with microphone inputs and speakers. It was essentially a PA system with a six-channel mixer to amplify the entire band and their instruments. This was at a time when most bands only had one mic—for the vocalist.

His work caught the attention of Leon Cam, who owned Cam's Electrical Appliances on Sargent Avenue in the city's West End. The shop sold everything from furniture and appliances to stereos, and also did radio and TV repairs. Gillies oversaw the latter side before eventually buying the business entirely. Selling appliances and furniture kept the bills paid, but Gillies's attention turned more to repairing and reconditioning old amplifiers and musical instruments.

In 1963, a tall, skinny kid named Neil Young wandered into the store. The future rock icon was with Kenny Koblun, the bass player from their Winnipeg band The Squires, according to a 2006 *Globe and Mail* article by Martin Patriquin.

Koblun needed a new bass and Young couldn't understand why they were going to a TV and refrigerator store. The discovery of what else

Gillies offered led to a long relationship between Young and Garnet amps. For Gillies, it marked a transition in his business, which began to focus more on his true love—music.

It was a time when Winnipeg's burgeoning rock scene meant hundreds of young musicians were playing at dozens of dances at city community centres.

It was a time when Winnipeg's burgeoning rock scene meant hundreds of young musicians were playing at dozens of dances at city community centres. The dances required music, and the musicians who played them needed somewhere to buy and repair their gear, wrote Patriquin. Gillies was happy to help.

Firsts in the Northwest 1959-1972

1959

At 12:01 a.m., Winnipeg's 999 emergency line goes live—the first three-digit emergency phone number in North America, nearly a decade before 911 is introduced.

Developed by the provincial Crown corporation Manitoba Telephone System, the service is credited with helping save eleven lives in just the first two years, due to the efficient response of emergency services.

Eight operators are initially hired, along with a supervisor, so the service can operate around the clock with two dispatch operators always on duty. The emergency centre is housed in Winnipeg's Central Police Station on Rupert Avenue.

The original nine staffers are all female, because women are paid less and Winnipeg wants to bring the cost down to get the other eleven municipalities surrounding the city to buy in. Those municipalities all have their own numbers for police, ambulance, fire, and poison control.

The idea of the unified emergency line is pitched by Winnipeg,

999 CALL CENTRE IN 1965 City of Winnipeg Archives

though there is resistance to the cost. Though it works out to just over 10 cents per person in each municipality, that is seen as extravagant by the more populous ones. Employing women instead of men cuts the cost by 25 per cent and the plan is accepted. Women get a monthly salary of $200, instead of the $345 men would have been given.

The centre initially averages 75 calls per day, a number that rises steadily. In a short time, it is about 300, as more people adapt to its use.

Even so, debate over the system continues until November 22, 1959. That's when 41-year-old Bernard Potter wakes up with a terrible headache, as does his wife. Moments later their 16-year-old son collapses at the foot of their bed.

As the family is being overcome by a gas leak from their new furnace, Potter manages to dial 999 and stay conscious long enough to mumble his address. All seven members of the Potter family are pulled from the home unconscious but alive.

Not only does the incident confirm the necessity of the line for city administrators, but it also catches the attention of other cities and leads to a system of dispatches across Canada.

In the US, the first three-digit number and call is made in Alabama in 1968. The number adopted there is 911, chosen because it has never been designated for an office code, area code, or service code. It is also seen as quicker than dialling three 9s on a rotary phone. Canada follows suit, making 911 the standard in 1972. The first city to implement the system is London, Ontario, in 1974. Winnipeg changes over in 1975.

By that time, Winnipeg has amalgamated with

Some of the first amps he built from scratch were small vacuum tube-based ones designed for Chad Allen and the Expressions, a group for which Gillies' son Russell was manager and roadie. As the group's popularity grew, so did the exposure to their amps and PA equipment, which meant an expanding list of customers for Gillies.

"And so we started building amplifiers. At no time had we planned to be Garnet amplifiers. It just evolved," Gillies told CBC News in a 2003 interview, three years before he died.

When Chad Allen and the Expressions released a cover of the British hit "Shakin' All Over" in 1965, the fortunes of the group—and those of Gillies—changed forever.

The song was a massive hit in the United States and Canada, but nobody initially knew it was them. The band's label sent the recording to radio stations with the playful question, Guess Who? It was a ploy to disguise the fact that the group was Canadian in the hope DJs would think it was another breakout band from the ongoing Beatles-led British Invasion.

Burton Cummings and his Garnet amp, 1966 COURTESY JOHN EINARSON

The band's actual name was released later, but DJs continued to call them Guess Who, so it stuck. The band officially adopted the name by the start of 1966. That's when the band started to experience some shakin' all over of its own. Future superstar Burton Cummings joined the band as keyboardist in January 1966 and two months later took over as lead singer when Chad Allen left. The Guess Who's popularity grew and they started to get bookings at bigger venues.

They also shifted to Fender-made amplifiers, moving on from the smaller ones from Gillies, but quickly found the Fenders couldn't provide the necessary volume. So Russell again turned to his dad.

Gillies boosted the band's amps with bigger vacuum tubes, according to Winnipeg music historian John Einarson. He built a custom-made portable public-address system for vocals and monster-sized (by 1966 standards) 100-watt amplifiers for the instruments.

"He beefed up Garnets with the most powerful tubes on the market, giving them extreme volume and a warmth only tubes could give," Einarson said.

Gillies sold the appliance and furniture business around 1967, after having moved it to the corner of Osborne Street and Morley Avenue in the South Osborne neighbourhood. He created the Garnet Amplifier Company, partnering with his two sons, Russell and Garnet, and coined the slogan "The Sound of The Pros" to market the powerful line of amps. They set up in a large shop on Ferry Road, near the airport, which served for both sales and manufacturing.

"They were the biggest amps available anywhere and provided the backdrop bands wanted—a wall of heavy sound." John Einarson

By 1968 nearly every band in the city had Garnet gear, whether the 50-watt Pro series or the 100-watt BTO (Big-Time Operator) line—the tallest, loudest amplifiers this side of the Atlantic Ocean, according to Einarson.

They were the biggest amps available anywhere and provided the backdrop bands wanted—a wall of heavy sound, Einarson said. The amps were augmented by columns of Garnet speakers that

Brochure for Garnet's BTO series of amps   GARNETAMPS.COM

---

its eleven surrounding municipalities.

1960

January: Olive Lillian Irvine becomes the first woman from the Prairies to be called to the Senate in Ottawa. She serves as a member of Senate committees on divorce, labour, public health, and welfare.

1961

October 1: Canada's first—and now largest—privately owned television network, CTV, is launched by Spencer "Spence" Wood Caldwell, a graduate of Winnipeg's Kelvin High School. Until then, network broadcasting was the sole domain of CBC.

Caldwell is a technology whiz kid whose first radio receiver is one he built himself. Shortly after graduating from Kelvin in the late 1920s, he lands a job with the Hudson's Bay Company in downtown Winnipeg, managing the store's new radio department.

He later joins the Montreal-based Marconi Company as their broadcast equipment sales manager for Western Canada, while continuing to live in Winnipeg. He moves to Toronto in the mid-1940s to become a network manager.

In 1958, the Board of Broadcast Governors— forerunner to the Canadian

Radio-television and Telecommunications Commission—is created as the governing body of Canadian broadcasting. It ends CBC's dual role as regulator and broadcaster. Soon afterwards, the BBG takes applications for the country's first privately owned TV stations. Caldwell is one of eight applicants but not chosen.

Undaunted, he aims higher. In April 1960, he pitches the idea of an entire network. He names it the Canadian Television Network (CTN). It takes months before the BBG grants the licence, and the network hits the air October 1, 1961. A year later the name is changed to the CTV Television Network, after CBC objects to the original moniker, arguing it has exclusive rights to use "Canadian" in its name.

Many think CTV stands for **C**anadian **T**ele**V**ision, but the letters actually have no official meaning.

1963

Dr. Frank Gunston is credited with inventing the world's first artificial knee.

Gunston was born in Flin Flon in 1933. As a boy in an isolated northern town in Manitoba, Gunston develops a mechanical proficiency, tinkering on cars and machining parts.

featured something no other company offered: driver horns that blasted out the vocals.

Garnet amps also had a built-in fuzz tone, called a stinger, that no other amp in North America offered. Typically, fuzz tones were created by standalone pedals placed between the guitar and amp that distorted sound.

When other musicians saw and heard The Guess Who's stage setup, they all craved the power and began ordering the gear. Soon there was a range of products from the smaller Rebel and Lil' Rock line of amps to the more powerful Pro and BTO.

Bachman, an innovator much like Gillies, had been experimenting with sound before the Guess Who emerged. During community centre gigs with Chad Allen, he would plug a smaller amp into a bigger one and crank the volume to create a unique sustained sound. Inevitably, it caused a meltdown of one or both amps. Repair shops turned him away, saying they couldn't fix the gear and he should stop overloading them. But Bachman found an ally in Gillies.

They began testing volume and effects at Gillies' warehouse in an industrial area of the city. Gillies then built a pre-amp able to replicate Randy's rich and growly tone without it causing anything to melt. The device boosted the signal into the amplifier, allowing the sound to overload, or overdrive, Einarson said.

According to Patriquin, Bachman was reading a book by German film director Werner Herzog, so Herzog became the name of the new pre-amp which created the distinctive buzz on songs like "No Time" and "American Woman."

The Guess Who soared to fame using Garnet gear exclusively and even recorded one of their songs, "Pretty Blues Eyes," in the

Gar Gillies, 1968
COURTESY
HANS SIPMA

BTO and Herzog amp combo
GARNETAMPS.COM

His first degree is in engineering, in 1957.

He's working as an engineer for Hudson Bay Mining and Smelting when the company sends him to England to work with the new technology of transistors. He becomes fascinated by its role in the pacemaker—another new technology.

He returns to Winnipeg and obtains his degree in medicine, graduating from the University of Manitoba specializing in orthopedics. He's on a fellowship in England in 1967, part of a travelling group that performs hip joint replacements, when he observes patients with arthritic pain in their knees.

His two passions come together when he designs the knee prosthesis. Up to then, treatment for arthritic knees is to fuse the bones. While it means no pain, it also means no flexibility. Gunston aims to copy the normal mechanism of the knee and uses a machine shop in England to make a prototype. He then perfects it on knee joints from cadavers. He goes on to install twenty-two artificial knees on patients in England before returning to Canada.

He could have patented his invention and made money through commercial development of the design. Instead, he publishes his work in a 1971 research paper, making the design available to anyone to copy and give people a chance to walk without pain.

He also goes to Finland and Switzerland to explain the designs before teaching at the U of M and in Winnipeg hospitals. He moves to Brandon in 1982 and practises orthopedics and joint replacement at Brandon General Hospital before retiring in 2000.

Gunston's design has been used as a template for modern variations and remains an integral part of the design of today's prosthetics.

1970
Josefina Asgerdur Kristjanson becomes the first woman to administer a veterans' hospital in Canada. A graduate of the University of Manitoba's Faculty of Medicine in 1943, she joins the medical staff of the Deer Lodge Hospital in Winnipeg in 1947, working as an allergy specialist. She becomes the hospital's assistant administrator in the early 1960s and then administrator in 1970. She is instrumental in the creation of the geriatric day hospital at the facility.

1972
The Winnipeg Art Gallery becomes the first public art gallery in Canada to display contemporary Indigenous art.

Ferry Road shop, with Gillies playing trombone on the track, according to Patriquin.

Bachman left the band in 1970, shortly after the release of *American Woman*, and formed his own band, Brave Belt. The name was later changed to BTO. Officially, it was an acronym for Bachman Turner Overdrive, but it was also a nod to Gillies' Big Time Operator amps.

The Guess Who on stage in 1968, bordered and backed by Garnet amps COURTESY HANS SIPMA

Gillies became known as Papa Gar to the musicians he supplied, always making himself available for a repair and quick turnaround.

For those who didn't have the cash to buy gear outright, Gillies was there.

"If you gave him five bucks a week or five bucks a month, he was happy. He gave every musician credit, something no one else gave us, and every band in Winnipeg is indebted to him for that attitude," Bachman told Patriquin.

SOUNDMAN HEROISM

Gillies was not only a hero to local bands. In 1971, Led Zeppelin was headlining the outdoor Man-Pop Festival at the old Winnipeg football stadium. A few hours before they were to take the stage, a storm blew through, tearing away the awning protecting the PA system and amps, which became drenched.

Organizers scrambled to relocate the festival into the nearby Winnipeg Arena. Gillies was called in to pull together a replacement PA system and by midnight had assembled what was needed to host the British supergroup.

The Guess Who perform in Winnipeg's Memorial Park, 1970. COURTESY HANS SIPMA

"Gar Gillies went down in the annals of sound-man heroism," wrote Patriquin.

Papa Gar gave everything to ensure music would be heard loud and clear—mostly loud. His largesse became legendary. Unfortunately, some took advantage. A few musicians never paid off their credit debts, which caused a financial squeeze for Gillies. But it was more his devotion to sound than generosity to friends that led to his downfall.

New technology emerged in place of the fragile glass cylinders that Gillies preferred to use in powering his electronic components. Semiconductors in the form of solid-state transistors were cheaper and more durable, but Gillies held off adopting them. He insisted they couldn't produce the same high-quality sound.

Sales of Garnet amplifiers dropped as retail outlets across Western Canada stopped stocking his gear. Gillies eventually, and reluctantly, made the transition but was behind competitors who were already well established in the new market.

To get back into the game, he struck a deal with US guitar giant Gibson to produce amps that would be sold under that brand. It was Garnet's first foray into solid state transistors. But it was a bad business deal for Gillies, according to Einarson, and ultimately brought Garnet to its knees. By the late 1980s, the shop on Ferry Road shut its doors.

Gillies later opened a small shop on St. Matthews Avenue in Winnipeg's West End, returning to his modest roots, tinkering with amplifiers and repairing old Garnets and other vacuum tube models. It was a low-key enterprise but kept him busy doing what he loved best, Einarson said. Some of his customers were devotees from the higher echelons of musicdom, the likes of Bachman, Cummings, Young, Gordie Johnson of Big Sugar, and Lenny Kravitz.

Gillies died in December 2006 after a year-long battle with bone cancer.

For years, a mural honouring Gillies stood tall and long, taking up the entire side of a building at the corner of Portage Avenue and Ashburn Street in Winnipeg's West End. Painted on a series of wood panels, it featured an oversized image of Gillies posing with a Garnet-emblazoned amp.

Tribute mural for Gar Gillies on building at corner of Portage Avenue and Ashburn Street in Winnipeg's West End. It includes a message from Randy Bachman that reads: *Thanks for 'The Sound' you gave me. It really made me stand out amongst other guitarists. You can stand proud knowing it helped every band in town. You are talked about often with love and thanks in our heart.* WEST END BIZ

A smaller image showed Gillies standing on an amp and playing trombone—a nod to his big band days. Another showed The Guess Who in concert. Near the big image of Gillies was a recreated handwritten message from Bachman: *Thanks for 'The Sound' you gave me. It really made me stand out amongst other guitarists. You can stand proud knowing it helped every band in town. You are talked about often with love and thanks in our heart. Love and Feedback. Randy Bachman.*

The mural was erected in 2003 on the side of Second Encore Music store, paid for by the owner and the West End BIZ. It came down mysteriously in the summer of 2019, the panels found piled up in the alley by Gillies' daughter, who called it disrespectful.

The music store had long moved out and two other businesses had come and gone in that time. According to a story by *Global News Winnipeg*, the current tenant, a travel agency, claimed it was taken down to be restored. It was retrieved by the West End BIZ, but the wall remains empty as of 2023.

Garnet amplifiers and Herzog pre-amps are now sought and treasured by collectors and have been exhibited as part of the National Music Centre's collection in Calgary. But the business itself has not vanished. It's being carried on by Pete Thiessen, a Winnipegger who purchased the rights to the company from Gillies in early 2006 and runs the website garnetamps.com.

Garnet amplifiers and Herzog pre-amps are now sought and treasured by collectors.

ROCK-OLA

Three decades before Gillies debuted his Garnets, another Manitoban with a penchant for sound and electronics began to juke his way into history.

With a name like David Rockola, the Virden-born innovator was destined for music distinction. And his name has been immortalized on every Rock-Ola jukebox since 1935.

Born in 1897, David Cullen Rockola learned early on to fend for himself. His parents split up when he was quite young and then his mother, with whom he lived along with three of his four brothers, died in 1911. At fourteen, he quit school, left his home, and hit the road to find work. He travelled across Canada taking various jobs, learning the merchant trade and growing street smart and business wise.

One of his first jobs was as a mechanic in a vending machine factory, which piqued his interest in coin-operated devices. He also worked briefly as a bellhop in Saskatoon, Saskatchewan, then, though still a teenager, at a hotel in Medicine Hat, Alberta, where he ran a cigar shop.

David Rockola showing off some of his early coin-operated gum machines ROCK-OLA1448.NL/HISTORY-ROCK-OLA

He recounted his time in Alberta during an interview in 1987 with a high school newspaper reporter in Indiana. Rockola said he became such an obsessive worker that he fell ill, contracted diphtheria and had to be hospitalized. "They took my cigar store away from me," he said.

After recovering and being discharged, Rockola moved to Calgary where he ran another cigar shop. It was there, according to a story on the Made-in-Chicago Museum website, that two men entered the store one day and sold him a gumball-type machine that dispensed prizes, including vouchers for items in the shop. Before long, the machine was more in demand than the cigars, and Rockola was hooked.

SLOT MACHINE SYNDICATE

In 1919, he crossed the border for the United States and ended up in Chicago, where he first worked as an inspector for a slot machine manufacturer, then as a mechanic for a company that built coin-operated amusement games, particularly pinball.

Around 1926, he and two partners started a small business dealing in penny scales that provided people's weight and often spit out a horoscope as well. Within a year, Rockola embarked on his own and launched the Rock-Ola Scale Co. He then expanded into slot machines, arcade games and pinball machines, gumball machines, and even parking meters, changing his business name to the Rock-Ola Manufacturing Co.

Along the way, Rockola became entangled with the criminal underworld, which rigged slot machines to short-change payouts, reaping profits that dodged taxes. Rockola supplied many of the machines to the so-called slot machine syndicate, according to the Made-in-Chicago Museum website.

David Rockola, left, before going into court with his lawyer Louis Piquette, 1929
MADE-IN-CHICAGO MUSEUM/
MADEINCHICAGOMUSEUM.COM

Rockola became entangled with the criminal underworld, which rigged slot machines to short-change payouts, reaping profits that dodged taxes.

In 1929, the Illinois state's attorney went after the slot machine racket and formed a grand jury to collect testimony. Rockola was among those who implicated mob bosses while admitting his involvement, which included paying off high-ranking officers.

His testimony built the bulk of the state's case, which ensnared gangsters, police, politicians, and people from the mayor's office—twenty-one defendants in all. He was granted immunity from prosecution, but Rockola knew how to play the game. When it came to the actual trial he leaned on the fifth amendment, the right to refuse to answer questions to avoid incriminating himself. That made it impossible for the state's attorney to proceed. All defendants were let off

Ads for two of Rock-Ola's early pinball games, Juggle Ball and Jigsaw   ROCK-OLA1448.NL/HISTORY-ROCK-OLA

the hook, except Rockola, who the judge found in contempt of court. He went to jail for six months, but the legal maneuvering kept him in the mob's good books.

MAGIC OF THE MULTI-SELECTOR

The following year business was stronger than ever and two of his pinball creations were part of the 1933 Chicago World's Fair, earning great exposure. By 1934, the Rock-Ola company moved into a massive 250,000-square-foot factory warehouse.

That's where Rockola made the biggest move of his life. The repeal of Prohibition in the US one year earlier led to a boom in taverns and

Rockola in front of his factory in Chicago MADE-IN-CHICAGO MUSEUM/MADEINCHICAGOMUSEUM.COM

nightclubs, and Rockola saw another opportunity: coin-operated music.

He met an inventor who developed a device with a mechanical arm that could pick a record out of a pile of discs, play it and return it back. Rockola bought the patent, re-engineered it and went into production.

The first jukebox, the twelve-record Multi-Selector, rolled off the assembly line in 1935 and became an immediate success. Other companies had been making phonograph players for several years, but they only allowed one song selection at a time. Rockola's machine allowed several choices to be logged. It would remember the sequence and play them in order, setting the blueprint for all jukeboxes to follow.

The Rock-Ola brand became synonymous with music and, because it predated the wide use of rock as a music genre, it led some to credit Rockola with inspiring the term. After all, it wasn't until 1951 that Cleveland disc jockey Alan Freed first referred to music that fused rhythm and blues and country as rock 'n roll, popularizing the term on mainstream radio.

The first jukebox, the twelve-record Multi-Selector, rolled off the assembly line in 1935 and became an immediate success.

But most historians agree the roots go back much further than that. The phrase had long been used by sailors to describe the literal "rocking and rolling" of a ship. Then it was commandeered as a metaphor for the undulating movements of dancing and sex. But it was also used for a spiritual and religious fervour. The earliest known recordings of the phrase date back the late 1890s in *The Camp Meeting Jubilee* song, with its lyrics, "Keep on rockin' an' rolling in your arms/ Rockin' an' rolling in your arms/ Rockin' an' rolling in your arms/ In the arms of Moses."

Rock-Ola jukebox ROCKOLA.CO.UK

ROCK-OLA
S·T·E·R·E·O·P·H·O·N·I·C all-purpose phonograph

tempo II

*Unmatched in brilliance of styling
Unequalled in proven dependability*

Model 1475

Rock-Ola might not have created rock, but it did help launch a musical and cultural revolution.

Rock-Ola might not have created rock, but it did help launch a musical and cultural revolution. It is also part and parcel with some significant moments in history. In 1936, a Rock-Ola player was part of the maiden voyage of the luxury liner *Queen Mary*. The celebrated ship arrived in New York from England in June and on its return, had a Multi-Selector entertaining guests.

As production of jukeboxes continued to expand and evolve, Rock-Ola began offering models with up to 60 records, meaning 120 song selections, and adapting to changing record sizes.

The introduction of plastics revolutionised the Rock-Ola look from wooden boxes to light-up cabinets covered with marbleized designs. The company also came up with a jukebox that could be hung on a wall and small versions that could sit on diner and cafe tables.

The demand for jukeboxes declined in the '70s and Rock-Ola's biggest—and last remaining—competitor, Wurlitzer, suspended production in 1974. At the time, there were some 600,000 Rock-Ola jukeboxes tucked away in bowling alleys, bars and coffeehouses throughout North and South America, according to the *Los Angeles Times*.

Rock-Ola kept rolling through the 1980s, venturing into video arcade machines and a hybrid jukebox that played both 45 rpm records and compact discs. The company was sold in 1992 to Glenn Streeter, owner of Antique Apparatus Co., who re-introduced many nostalgic designs from his factory in California. Rock-Ola was sold again, in July 2019, to Alexander Walder-Smith, owner of The Games Room Company based in the United Kingdom.

David Rockola died in Chicago in January 1993, three days after turning 96. He was posthumously inducted into the Amusement Industry Hall of Fame in 2023.

A model '1428' Rock-Ola jukebox is displayed in the Library of Congress on Capitol Hill in Washington, DC as an example of Americana.

Rock-Ola continues to be the last remaining jukebox manufacturer in North America.

There were some 600,000 Rock-Ola jukeboxes tucked away in bowling alleys, bars and coffeehouses throughout North and South America.

CHURCHILL'S MISSING GRAVITY

It has the world's largest concentration of polar bears, thousands of curious and sociable beluga whales, and night skies that erupt in surges and sways of emerald and pink aurora.

Churchill sits at the confluence of three major biomes: marine, boreal forest and tundra, with each supporting a variety of flora and fauna. It's a birdwatcher's paradise with some 270 species recorded.

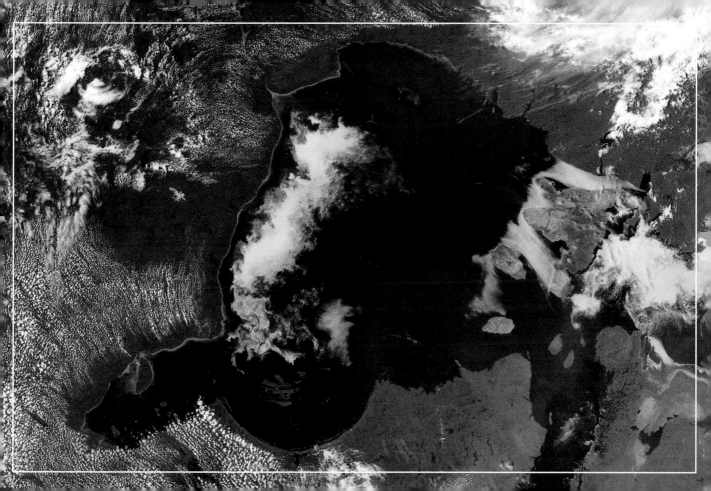

Canons left in ruins of Prince of Wales Fort, circa 1930s
PROVINCIAL ARCHIVES OF MANITOBA, FILE F-49

Names carved in Sloot Cove rocks PROVINCIAL ARCHIVES OF MANITOBA, P1173

Just across the Churchill River, on the last spit of land before terrain gives way to the brackish deep of the vast Hudson Bay, stands a 250-year-old national historic site—the stone-built, star-shaped Prince of Wales Fort. The Historic Monuments Board of Canada says its ruins are "among the most interesting military remains on this continent."

And not far from that is the Sloop Cove, a sheltered nook off the river that served as a safe harbour and winter haven for Hudson's Bay Company ships. Iron rings driven into the rocks in the 1700s to moor the vessels can still be seen, along with inscriptions carved into the stone by explorers, including one by a twenty-two-year-old Samuel Hearne in 1767.

Churchill has many attractions, but there is one where it comes up light. That is, the actual force of attraction—gravity.

Polar bears don't hover over the tundra but they, and everything else in the Hudson Bay region (northernmost reaches of Manitoba, Ontario and Quebec, and southeast Nunavut), weigh slightly less than they would almost anywhere else on the planet. Specifically, about a tenth of an ounce less.

It's tiny, not really noticeable to the average person. But for scientists the anomaly is huge, and it took almost fifty years to understand it.

They first noticed it in the 1960s, when the planet's global gravity fields were charted during the infancy of satellite geodesy—the measurement of the form and dimensions of Earth.

Gravity is the mutual attraction between matter, and its strength is proportional to mass and distance. In a nutshell—without venturing into spacetime and the fabric of the universe—more mass means more gravitational force. The force weakens as distance between objects increases.

Earth's gravity pulls objects toward its centre, but the strength of that attraction varies because the

Aerial of Fort Prince of Wales. Date unknown.

planet's mass is not spread out proportionally. It also changes over time. Oceans and trenches, mountains, rivers, valleys, and plains all have disparate extents of mass and so, different gravitational pulls.

Earth's gravity pulls objects toward its centre, but the strength of that attraction varies because the planet's mass is not spread out proportionally.

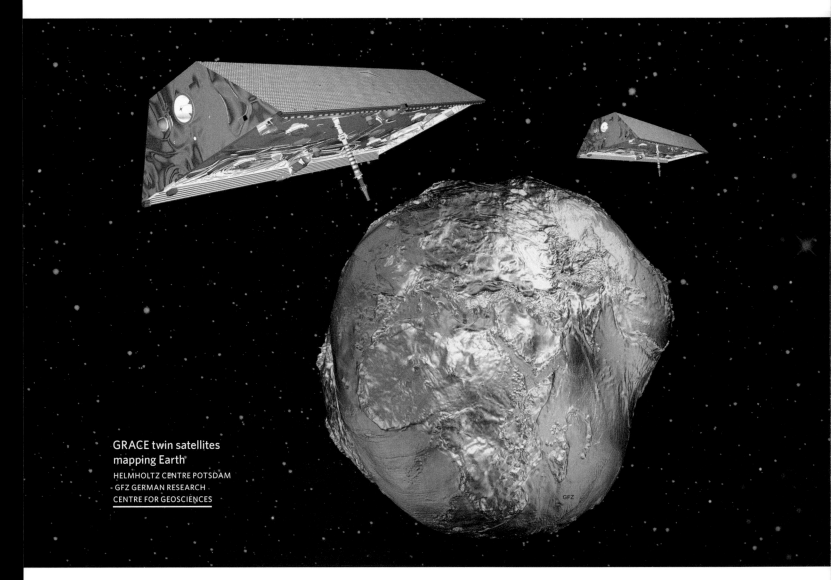

GRACE twin satellites
mapping Earth
HELMHOLTZ CENTRE POTSDAM
- GFZ GERMAN RESEARCH
CENTRE FOR GEOSCIENCES

The Earth is also not perfectly round. It looks more like a ball of cookie dough before it is baked, lumpy at random places and bulging at its mid-section due to centrifugal force from its rotation. As such, gravity is weaker at the equator because those areas are further from the core. But none of that applies to Churchill, so what gives?

The answer comes courtesy of satellites and technology that has vastly improved since the 1960s. The Gravity Recovery and Climate Experiment—GRACE—was a joint mission of NASA and the German Aerospace Center between March 2002 and October 2017.

Twin satellites, each weighing around 600 kilograms, circled the Earth during those fifteen years, mapping the planet's distribution of mass and corresponding gravity. They were able to provide global coverage of the gravity field every thirty days.

As the satellites went through their cycle, any slight variation in their orbit was measured. As one approached an area of greater mass, it acceler-ated and deviated closer to Earth, then it slowed and ascended as gravity's grip weakened. Though 220 kilometres apart, the satellites could calculate an adjustment between them as tiny as a micron, giving them a level of precision a hundred times greater than anything before.

The satellites were developed and built by French aerospace company Airbus (the same one that makes passenger airplanes) and the German Research Centre for Geosciences (GFZ). The data they recorded was used to create three-dimen-sional models of Earth with colours representing variations in the gravity field.

The colours range from red (strongest gravity), through yellow to blue (weakest). What the map-ping found was a handful of blue spots around the globe, including one centred over Churchill. The blue spots became known as gravity holes.

10,000-YEAR-OLD INDENT

When a GRACE satellite would fly over Churchill or other Hudson Bay regions, a decrease in gravi-tational pull allowed it to move further from

Firsts in the Northwest 1993-2023

1993

March 5: W. Yvon Dumont is sworn in as the lieutenant-governor of Manitoba, the first Métis person in Canadian history to hold a vice-regal office.

1994

November 8: Aboriginal Veterans Day is founded in Winnipeg. It has since spread nationwide as a day of observance to honour the thousands of First Nations, Métis and Inuit who served in the Canadian Armed Forces.

According to Veterans Affairs Canada, more than 12,000 Indigenous people served in the First and Second World Wars, as well as in Korea. But until the turn of the millennium, those veterans were denied the services and support—including land and educational benefits—provided to non-Indigenous vets. Indigenous veterans were also prohibited from participating in Remembrance Day services as a group, or lay wreaths.

In defiance, they created their own day of honour in Winnipeg. It is now celebrated as National Indigenous Veterans Day.

Earth. Scientists believe there are two reasons for the gravity anomaly there: the ancient imprint of ice, and convection in the Earth's core.

Hudson Bay—the second largest bay in the world—was once buried under the centre of one of the largest glaciers in history. The Laurentide Ice Sheet covered much of present-day Canada and the northern United States. The sheet began forming some 75,000 years ago and reached a peak about 20,000 years ago. Its thickness was just over three kilometres in general, but closer to four kilometres at Hudson Bay. The sheer weight compressed the Earth's crust. It carved the landscape through cycles of growth and melt, gouging out the Great Lakes and sculpting valleys. When the ice pushed down, it crushed and shoved mounds of rock far out, to the edges of its reach. Imagine pressing your hand into wet sand. The area taking the brunt is forced down while the edges are pushed up and away.

As Earth started to warm, the ice sheet shrunk, retreating north until it all but disappeared 10,000 years ago. The Barnes Ice Cap, in the middle of

Baffin Island in northern Canada, is the last visible remnant.

The ice left a deep indentation in the Earth that took thousands of years to recover. Since the Hudson Bay region was among the last to emerge from under the ice—and endured the thickest section—the effects are still being felt. The land is still rebounding like extremely slow memory foam—less than half an inch per year or about a metre per century.

Less mass in the area means less gravity. And it will be that way for a long time to come. It's estimated the Earth's crust has to rebound about 200 metres to return to its original state. That could take 5,000 years, scientists say.

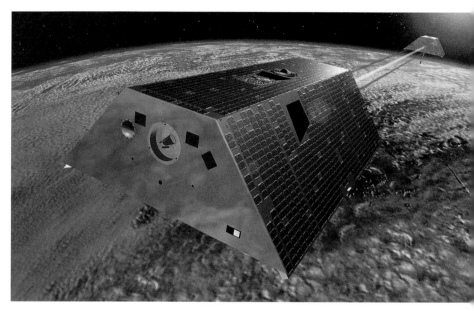

GRACE satellites communicating HELMHOLTZ CENTRE POTSDAM - GFZ GERMAN RESEARCH CENTRE FOR GEOSCIENCES

"We are able to show that the ghost of the ice age still hangs over North America," geophysicist Jerry Mitrovica told news website *Live Science* in 2007. Mitrovica, who was then at the University of Toronto and is now in the Department of Earth and Planetary Sciences at Harvard University, was part of a team that published a study about the imprint theory in the May 2007 issue of the journal *Science*. The study was based on GRACE data gathered between 2002 and 2006.

1998

October 28: Winnipeggers elect Glen Murray, Canada's first openly gay mayor.

2014

September 20: Canadian Museum for Human Rights opens to the public at The Forks in Winnipeg. It is the first national museum to be built outside of the national capital region of Ottawa.

2016

December 15: Jollibee, a fast-foot restaurant hailed as the McDonald's of the Philippines, opens in Winnipeg to long lineups on a frigid morning. It is the first Canadian location for the franchise, known for its Yumburger, Jolly Spaghetti, and Chickenjoy.

2023

October 3: The NDP is elected as the new government in Manitoba and leader Wabanakwut "Wab" Kinew becomes the first Indigenous person to be premier of a Canadian province.

Wab Kinew is seen on the day he was sworn in as Manitoba's first First Nations premier, Oct. 18, 2023. PRABHJOT SINGH LOTEY/CBC

The rebound effect around Hudson Bay can also be measured by other geological changes. Although sea levels around the globe are rising with climate change, the levels around Churchill and the Hudson Bay coast are lowering as the land rises.

In Sloop Cove in 1750, the water level was about three metres higher than today, according to Parks Canada. So the remnant iron rings fastened to the shoreline when Fort Prince of Wales was first built now sit well above the tidal level and the cove is now more of a meadow than a harbour.

Sloop Cove circa 1930s PROVINCIAL ARCHIVES OF MANITOBA, FILE F-49

CONVECTION AND SUBDUCTION

The ice imprint theory, however, only accounts for about half of the absent gravity in Manitoba's north. Scientists believe the process of convection within the Earth's mantle is responsible for the other half.

The mantle lies anywhere from five kilometres to 100 kilometres below the planet's crust, depending on whether measuring from the ocean floor or continental areas. It extends about 650 kilometres to the super-heated outer core and has a temperature range of 227 C at the crust boundary to nearly 4,000 C at the core boundary.

The molten rock of the mantle is churning and shifting, rising and falling, creating circulating currents of convection that pull down tectonic plates and alter the distribution of mass in parts of the world, including Churchill and Hudson Bay.

Convection currents transfer hot, buoyant magma to hot spots like the Yellowstone geyser, while pushing denser, cooler material from the crust to Earth's interior through the process of subduction. Hot spots tend to have high gravity, and cold ones, like Churchill, tend to have lower gravity.

All this to say, Churchill is unique for many reasons, most of which are clearly evident, but others that are less tangible. Visit for the history and manifest attractions without fear of floating away. You won't notice a thing in that regard; the phenomenon is real, but its effect is far too subtle, and the process is far too slow.

Adult polar bear with two cubs
SUSANNE MILLER, U.S. FISH AND WILDLIFE SERVICE

Focus instead on the polar bears. They are not slow. They have a lot of mass and will certainly notice you.

One cannot emphasize enough the gravity of that situation.

ACKNOWLEDGMENTS

Writing a book should be considered a team sport.

Short of having a time machine to visit historical events in person, an author relies on a network of people past and present, who often put in leviathan efforts, to find that information in the depths of archives and time.

I can't express enough gratitude for the wonderful folks at archives, museums and heritage institutions large and small. They are the guardians of history, ensuring images, videos, documents, maps, etc. are there for generations to discover and learn.

The following organizations willingly and warmly shared their collections and knowledge: Le Musée de Saint-Boniface and the St. Boniface Historical Society/Société historique de Saint-Boniface, the Transcona Museum, the Whyte Museum of the Canadian Rockies, and The Muse—Lake of the Woods Museum & Douglas Family Art Centre.

Manitobans are fortunate to have access to incredible digital collections through Winnipeg in Focus (City of Winnipeg Archives), PastForward (Winnipeg Public Library), the University of Manitoba Archives & Special Collections, Heritage Winnipeg, Winnipeg Architecture Foundation and the Western Canada Pictorial Index, and nationally at the Library and Archives Canada. I unapologetically spend far too much time exploring them all.

I am particularly indebted to the staff at the Archives of Manitoba, who can find a pin in a field of haystacks. And to facility manager Gilbert Badajos, who gave me a tour of the archives/former civic auditorium. He took me through the depths and heights of the building and through secret hallways walled off long ago.

The online search engine for the Manitoba Archives is a nightmare, but the staff are a dream. The hours they are open could be more convenient, too, but hey, expecting a government to spend money on heritage is less productive than actually building a time machine.

Murray Peterson, the City of Winnipeg's historical buildings officer, magically produces things I can't find elsewhere. And he's always quick with a response, as if he's waiting on my emails, which I would love to think is true but is unquestionably not.

Murray has also done his own share of writing about Canadian history, its people, buildings and important events. For keeping those stories in the light, I also offer my thanks as an appreciative fan.

If it weren't for Gordon Goldsborough, Christian Cassidy, Jim Smith, and John Einarson, most of my stories would be mere briefs and with few images. They have done so much to preserve the stories of Manitoba and Prairie history. It's all out of passion, and it shows. I am honoured to call them friends

As always, the Manitoba Historical Society is a resource whose value is beyond measurable calculation. In spite of a lean budget and scant staff, it offers immensely rich content on its website. No amount of applause comes close to the level of appreciation I feel for the MHS, which turns 145 in 2024 and is the oldest organization of its kind in Western Canada.

For bringing my stories into crisp focus, I thank the fine editing skills of Catharina de Bakker and the design genius of Relish Ideas Inc.

Finally, a great big thank-you to Great Plains Press for having confidence in me—twice now—and allowing me to share these stories.

CITATIONS

THE BELLS OF ST. BONIFACE

Balado Decouverte. "Cathédrale de Saint-Boniface: Inside the ruins of the previous cathedral."

Balado Discovery, June 18, 2022. https://baladodiscovery.com/circuits/836/poi/9584/cathedrale-de-saint-boniface

Bernhardt, Darren. "'Absolute Horror': Witnesses Cried as Fire Consumed St. Boniface Cathedral 50 Years Ago." cbc.ca, July 22, 2018. https://www.cbc.ca/news/canada/manitoba/st-boniface-cathedral-fire-anniversary-winnipeg-1.4748941.

Cathedral de St Boniface/ St Boniface Cathedral: cathedralestboniface.ca

Cherney, Bruce "St. Boniface Cathedral fires—basilica fire in 1860 started when tallow spilled on stove." *Winnipeg Regional Real Estate News*, October 30, 2008.

City of Winnipeg Historical Buildings Committee. *190 Avenue de la cathedrale- St. Boniface Cathedral,* Winnipeg: City of Winnipeg, September 2012.

Encyclopedia of French Cultural Heritage in North America: ameriquefrancaise.org

Faith ND, n.d. "St. Boniface." University of Notre Dame. https://faith.nd.edu/s/1210/faith/interior.aspx?sid=1210&gid=609&calcid=53508&calpgid=61&pgid=14866&crid=0

Girard, David. n.d. "The Cathedrals of Saint-Boniface." *Encyclopedia of French Cultural Heritage in North America.* http://www.ameriquefrancaise.org/en/article-621/the_cathedrals_of_saint-boniface.html

Le Musee de St Boniface/St Boniface Museum: msbm.mb.ca

Loyola Press. n.d. "Saint Boniface." https://www.loyolapress.com/catholic-resources/saints/saints-stories-for-all-ages/saint-boniface

MacLeod, Margaret Arnett. *Bells of the Red River.* Winnipeg: Stovel Company Ltd., 1937.

Manitoba Historical Society. "Historic Sites of Manitoba: St. Boniface Cathedral." Mhs.mb.ca, Last updated February 23, 2024. https://www.mhs.mb.ca/docs/sites/stbonifacecathedral.shtml

Province of Manitoba Historic Resources Branch. n.d. "Manitoba Provincial Heritage Site No. 80, St. Boniface Cathedral." https://www.gov.mb.ca/chc/hrb/prov/p080.html

Siamandas, George. "The St. Boniface Cathedral Fire" Winnipeg Time Machine (blog), February 1, 2007. https://winnipegtimemachine.blogspot.com/search?q=st+boniface+cathedral

Société historique de Saint-Boniface/St. Boniface Historical Society: https://shsb.mb.ca

Tourism Winnipeg, n.d. "St. Boniface Cathedral-Basilica." https://www.tourismwinnipeg.com/things-to-do/attractions/display,listing/06147/st-boniface-cathedral-basilica

THE FLOWER-BEARING AMERICAN SPY

Bowsfield, Hartwell. *The James Wickes Taylor Correspondence 1859–1870, Volume III*, general editor W. D. Smith. Altona: Manitoba Record Society Publications, 1968.

Bowsfield, Hartwell. "Taylor, James Wickes." in *Dictionary of Canadian Biography*, vol. 12, University of Toronto/Université Laval, 2003–, accessed June 13, 2024, http://www.biographi.ca/en/bio/taylor_james_wickes_12E.htm

Caryopsis, Johnny. n.d "Our Prairie Crocus: Crocus Day!" Naturenorth.com. http://www.naturenorth.com/spring/flora/crocus/Prairie_Crocus3.html

Craig, Irene. "The Crocus-Loving Consul." *Manitoba Pageant*, Vol. 7, No. 1 (September 1961). https://www.mhs.mb.ca/docs/pageant/07/crocuslovingconsul.shtml

MacBeth, R.G. "A Famous American Consul." *The Winnipeg Evening Tribune*, November 22, 1924.

Manitoba Historical Society. "Memorable Manitobans: James Wickes Taylor." mhs.mb.ca, May 19, 2018. https://www.mhs.mb.ca/docs/people/taylor_jw.shtml

Mindess, Mary. "The American That Winnipeggers Loved." *Winnipeg Free Press*, November 14, 1964.

Provincial Department of Industry and Commerce, Bureau of Travel and Publicity. *City of The Rivers*, Winnipeg, 1957.

Rea, J.E., and Jeff Scott. "Manitoba Act." *The Canadian Encyclopedia*. Historica Canada. Article published February 07, 2006; Last Edited January 07, 2021. https://www.thecanadianencyclopedia.ca/en/article/manitoba-act

Sandusky Library. "James W. Taylor: The American That Canadians Loved." Sandusky History (blog), April 25, 2009. https://sanduskyhistory.blogspot.com/2009/04/james-w-taylor-american-that-canadians.html

Wells, Eric. *Manitoba Nuggets*. Winnipeg: Royal Trust, 1978.

REPUBLIC OF MANITOBAH

Bowsfield, Hartwell. "Pioneer Politicking." *Manitoba Pageant*, Vol. 4, No. 3 (April 1959). https://www.mhs.mb.ca/docs/pageant/04/politicking.shtml

Bowsfield, Hartwell. "The Republic of Manitobah." *Manitoba Pageant*, Vol. 7, No. 1 (September 1961). https://www.mhs.mb.ca/docs/pageant/07/republicofmanitobah.shtml

Chafe, James Warren. *Extraordinary Tales from Manitoba History*, Winnipeg: Manitoba Historical Society in association with McClelland and Stewart Ltd., 1973.

Cherney, Bruce. "Short-lived Republic of Manitobah ends when shots are fired." *Winnipeg Regional Real Estate News*, October 2004.

Government of Manitoba, Department of Sport, Culture, Heritage, and Tourism. n.d. "Origin of the name Manitoba." https://www.gov.mb.ca/chc/ourdept/origin_name_manitoba.html

Hall, Frank. "How Manitoba Got Its Name." *Manitoba Pageant,* Vol. 15, No. 2 (Winter 1970). https://www.mhs.mb.ca/docs/pageant/15/manitobaname1.shtml

Hall, Frank. "Spirits of our past: Manitoba's history as seen through the bottom of a bottle." *Winnipeg Free Press,* November 7, 2020.

Manitoba Historical Society. "Lake Manitoba Narrows (Municipality of West Interlake)." mhs.mb.ca, last updated November 27, 2023. https://www.mhs.mb.ca/docs/sites/lakemanitobanarrows.shtml

Manitoba Historical Society. "Memorable Manitobans: Thomas Spence." mhs.mb.ca, last updated April 10, 2024. https://www.mhs.mb.ca/docs/people/spence_t.shtml.

SECRETS OF THE CIVIC AUDITORIUM

"Auditorium's supports dig deep in earth." *The Winnipeg Evening Tribune,* October 15, 1932.

Carter, Casimir. "Winnipeg Auditorium." *The Canadian Encyclopedia*. Historica Canada. Article published February 07, 2006; Last Edited July 04, 2014. https://www.thecanadianencyclopedia.ca/en/article/winnipeg-auditorium-emc

Government of Manitoba, Department of Sport, Culture, Heritage, and Tourism.n.d. "Manitoba Archives Building." https://www.gov.mb.ca/chc/archives/visiting/mb_archives_building.html

Heritage Winnipeg. "A Keystone of Culture: The Manitoba Museum." Heritage Winnipeg Blog, June 9, 2021. https://heritagewinnipeg.com/blogs/a-keystone-of-culture-the-manitoba-museum/

Macdonald, Catherine. *A City at Leisure: An illustrated history of parks and recreation services in Winnipeg*, Winnipeg: City of Winnipeg Parks and Recreation Department, 1995.

Manitoba Historical Society. "Historic Sites of Manitoba: Hudson's Bay Company Building." Mhs.mb.ca. Last updated April 29, 2023. https://www.mhs.mb.ca/docs/sites/hudsonsbaywinnipeg.shtml

Manitoba Historical Society. "Winnipeg Auditorium/Archives of Manitoba/Manitoba Legislative Library." Mhs.mb.ca. last updated February 23, 2024. https://mhs.mb.ca/docs/sites/winnipegauditorium.shtml

Nash, Knowlton. *Kennedy and Diefenbaker: Fear and Loathing Across the Undefended Border*, Toronto: McClelland & Stewart, 1990.

Smith, Denis. *Rogue Tory: The Life and Legend of John Diefenbaker*, Macfarlane Walter & Ross, 1995.

Winnipeg Architecture Foundation. n.d. "Civic Auditorium." Winnipegarchitecture.ca. https://winnipegarchitecture.ca/winnipeg-civic-auditorium

Winnipeg's Auditorium in the centre of Canada, 1932 souvenir booklet, Provincial Archives of Manitoba.

"Winnipeg Auditorium to open on Oct. 15 with big industrial exhibition." *Winnipeg Free Press,* September 3, 1932.

Young, Graham. *Collections and Research: The Old Museum Lives On*, Manitoba Museum blog, January 31, 2013.

THE MAN WHO SAVED THE BISON

Baird, Craig. "The Decline of the Bison." Canadian History Ehx. June 17, 2020. https://canadaehx.com/2020/06/17/the-decline-of-the-bison/

Brawn, Charles and Dale Brown. "Cell-block tee-off." *Brandon Sun*, September 13, 2007.

Campbell, Tim. "A game for the ages." *Winnipeg Free Press*, August 15, 2015.

Chafe, James Warren. *Extraordinary Tales from Manitoba History*, Winnipeg: Manitoba Historical Society in association with McClelland and Stewart Ltd., 1973.

Cherney, Bruce. "Buffalo hunt—great slaughter by hide hunters was 'stupendous' and short-sighted." *Winnipeg Regional Real Estate News*, September 9, 2011.

Cherney, Bruce. "Early days of golf—the first course in Manitoba was laid out by Stony Mountain's warden." *Winnipeg Real Estate News*, August 3, 2010.

Drysdale, Helen. "Manitoba Bison." *Neepawa Banner and Press*, March 12, 2021.

Frasier, Rhonda. n.d. "Charles Alloway." All About Bison. https://allaboutbison.com/bison-in-history/charles-alloway

Frasier, Rhonda. n.d. "Howard Eaton." All About Bison. https://allaboutbison.com/bison-in-history/howard-eaton/

Gibson, Lee. "Bedson, Samuel Lawrence." in *Dictionary of Canadian Biography*, vol. 12, University of Toronto/Université Laval, 2003–, accessed June 13, 2024. http://www.biographi.ca/en/bio/bedson_samuel_lawrence_12E.html.

Government of Manitoba, Historic Resources Branch. *Manitoba Heritage Council Commemorative Plaques: Silver Heights.* https://www.gov.mb.ca/chc/hrb/plaques/plaq1088.html

Hackett, Al. "Golf Introduced into Manitoba: Samuel Bedson and a Link at Stony Mountain." *Manitoba History Magazine*, No. 28 (Autumn 1994). https://www.mhs.mb.ca/docs/mb_history/28/manitobagolf.shtml

Healy, William James. *Winnipeg's Early Days*. Winnipeg: Stovel Company Ltd.,1927.

Historic Resources Branch Pamphlets. *Silver Heights*. Winnipeg: Manitoba Department of Cultural Affairs and Historical Resources, 1983- last updated May 26, 2023. https://www.mhs.mb.ca/docs/hrb/silverheights.shtml

"History recorded of Stony Mountain." *The Winnipeg Tribune*, January 7, 1961.

Lothian, W.F. *Parks Canada: A History of Canada's National Parks, Volume IV, Chapter 7 Preserving Canada's Wildlife*, Ottawa: Parks Canada, 1987.

Manitoba Historical Society. "Memorable Manitobans: Samuel Lawrence Bedson." mhs.mb.ca, April 26, 2022. https://www.mhs.mb.ca/docs/people/bedson_sl.shtml

Markewicz, Lauren. *Like Distant Thunder: Canada's Bison Conservation Story*, Ottawa: Parks Canada, 2017. https://parks.canada.ca/pn-np/ab/elkisland/nature/eep-sar/bison

Neufeld, Peter Lorenz. "Bison Conservation: The Canadian Story." *Manitoba History Magazine*, No. 24 (Autumn 1992). https://www.mhs.mb.ca/docs/mb_history/24/bisonconservation.shtml

Overby, Jillian. n.d. *History of Bison: From A Manitoba Perspective*, Manitoba Bison Association. https://www.manitobabison.ca/history-of-bison

Parks Canada. *Plains Bison Reintroduction: Wild bison return to Canada's first national park*. Ottawa: Government of Canada, last updated March 14, 2024. https://parks.canada.ca/pn-np/ab/banff/info/gestion-management/bison

"Silver Heights, the former residence of Lord Strathcona, is where the city kept its herd." *The Morning Telegram*, May 3, 1902.

Stephen, Scott. "James McKay (1828-1879): Métis Trader, Guide, Interpreter and MLA." *Manitoba History Magazine*, No. 58 (June 2008). https://www.mhs.mb.ca/docs/mb_history/58/mckay_j.shtml

Turner, Allan R. "McKay, Jame." in *Dictionary of Canadian Biography*, vol. 10, University of Toronto/Université Laval, 2003–, accessed June 13, 2024. http://www.biographi.ca/en/bio/mckay_james_10E.html

Whyte Museum of the Canadian Rockies. n.d. "Bringing Back the Buffalo: The Pablo-Allard herd and the reintroduction of buffalo to the Canadian plains." https://www.explore.whyte.org/buffalo

WHEN KENORA WAS IN MANITOBA … AND ONTARIO

Association of Manitoba Land Surveyors. n.d. *The First Boundary Extension*. https://amls.ca/wp-content/uploads/2023/02/amls_The-first-boundary-extension-New.pdf

Barr, Elinor. "Kenora." *The Canadian Encyclopedia*. Historica Canada. Article published October 22, 2012; Last Edited December 21, 2022. https://www.thecanadianencyclopedia.ca/en/article/kenora

Britannica, T. Editors of Encyclopaedia. "Kenora." *Encyclopedia Britannica*, June 9, 2024. https://www.britannica.com/place/Kenora.

Burchill, John. *The Rat Portage War*. Winnipeg: Winnipeg Police Museum, 2021. https://winnipegpolicemuseum.ca/wp-content/uploads/2021/03/the-rat-portage-war.pdf

Chafe, James Warren. *Extraordinary Tales from Manitoba History*, Winnipeg: Manitoba Historical Society in association with McClelland and Stewart Ltd., 1973.

Cherney, Bruce. "The Rat Portage War—Ontario and Manitoba clash over town now called Kenora." *Winnipeg Regional Real Estate News*. October 3, 2008.

Grace Anne II. n.d. *History of the Area: The Western Waterway*. https://www.graceanne.com/location/history-of-the-area

Historical Review of Rat Portage and Lake of the Woods to commemorate Jubilee Jamboree Celebration, June 28th to July 1st, 1952. Kenora, 1952.

Kemp, Douglas. "From Postage Stamp to Keystone." *Manitoba Pageant*, April 1956. https://www.mhs.mb.ca/docs/pageant/01/boundaries.shtml

Ontario Heritage Trust. n.d. "Rat Portage Post." https://www.heritagetrust.on.ca/plaques/rat-portage-post

Retson, James C. n.d. *The Story of Kenora.* https://retson.ca/kenora.html

Sunset Country Travel Association. "History of Kenora, Ontario, Canada." https://visitsunsetcountry.com/history-of-kenora-ontario-canada

Wells, Eric. *Manitoba Nuggets.* Winnipeg: Royal Trust, 1978.

BERGEN CUTOFF: THE PATH OF UNFULFILLED PROMISES

"Big plans for old bridge." *Free Press Weekly*, December 11, 1988.

Campbell, Alex. "The Bergen Cut-Off" *Manitoba Co-operator*, June 7, 2017. https://www.manitobacooperator.ca/country-crossroads/rail-bridge-in-winnipeg-a-historical-remnant-of-a-forgotten-grain-line/

"City hopes for legal snags in railway bridge sale." *Winnipeg Free Press*, June 15, 1987.

"City to seek use of railway bridge." *Winnipeg Free Press*, August 28, 1953.

"City to vote on 1 bridge–midtown." *Winnipeg Free Press*, September 9, 1953.

"CPR dismisses 328 employees today." *Manitoba Free Press*, December 15, 1928.

"CPR won't sell or lease Bergen Cutoff." *Winnipeg Free Press*, October 20, 1953.

Dawson, Allan. "Thunder Bay—Manitoba's grain port?" *Manitoba Co-operator*, December 30, 2020. https://www.manitobacooperator.ca/news-opinion/news/thunder-bay-manitobas-grain-port/

"Developer makes case for Bergen Cutoff." *Winnipeg Free Press*, April 25, 1987.

Kemp, Dave. "Who is responsible for Perimeter bridge? Metro will meet with Roblin for talks on bridge spending." *The Winnipeg Tribune*, November 3, 1962.

"Kildonan residents battle riverbank developers." *Winnipeg Free Press*, March 7, 1987.

Manitoba Historical Society. "Historic Sites of Manitoba: Canadian Pacific Railway Bergen Cutoff Bridge." Mhs.mb.ca. Last updated July 27, 2023. https://www.mhs.mb.ca/docs/sites/bergencutoffbridge.shtml

Manitoba Historical Society. "Historic Sites of Manitoba: Canadian Pacific Railway North Transcona Grain Elevator." Mhs.mb.ca. Last updated October 11, 2021. https://www.mhs.mb.ca/docs/sites/northtransconaelevator.shtml

Manitoba Historical Society. "Historic Sites of Manitoba: Canadian Pacific Railway North Transcona Yard." Mhs.mb.ca. Last updated January 14, 2024. https://www.mhs.mb.ca/docs/sites/cprnorthtransconayard.shtml

Martin, Nick. "Fore! Golf club touted—for an old city bridge." *Winnipeg Free Press*, March 21, 1994.

"Neighbours outraged: Bergen Cut-off development threatens green space." *Free Press Weekly,* April 9, 1989.

"Plans for eatery suspended." *Winnipeg Free Press*, April 24, 1988.

"Plea to CPR: Bergen cutoff wanted for Metro road." *Winnipeg Free Press*, February 14, 1964.

Redekop, Bill. "Bootleg empire launched in CNR shops; Excerpt from Crimes of the Century: Manitoba's Most Notorious True Crimes." *Winnipeg Free Press Magazine*, December 1, 2002.

Santin, Aldo. "Development plan upsets residents, North Kildonan neighbours fear trail will be bulldozed." *Winnipeg Free Press,* July 20, 2003.

Smith, Jim. "The story of North Transcona School." *Winnipeg Free Press Community Review*, April 27, 2022.

Tizzard, Ian. "Dreamin' High: Rail bridge planner patiently continues 20-year wait." *Winnipeg Free Press*, July 7, 2007.

"Tram-Track issue stirs 'playing politics' charge." *Winnipeg Free Press*, October 22, 1953.

Transcona ad. *The Voice newspaper*, University of Manitoba digital collections, May 10, 1912, p7

Transcona Museum. "Communities that time forgot: North Transcona." May 5, 2018. https://www.transconamuseum.mb.ca/post/2017/11/18/communities-that-time-forgot-north-transcona

Winnipeg Architecture Foundation. n.d. "Landscape Architects: Garry Hilderman 1940–2016." https://winnipegarchitecture.ca/garry-hilderman

FUGITIVE TO FOLK HERO: SHOOTOUTS, HIDEOUTS AND MANHUNTS FOR PERCY MOGGEY

"11 months of freedom ends for Percy Moggey." *The Brandon Sun*, June 12, 1961.

"A sentimental shrine to a favourite fugitive: Bank robber's hideout to be tourist attraction." *Winnipeg Free Press,* May 2, 1998.

"Additional prison terms given two jail-breakers." *Winnipeg Free Press*, May 26, 1949.

"All-night city search for Moggey in vain." *Winnipeg Free Press*, August 8, 1960.

"Arrests follow Man Street gun fight." *The Winnipeg Tribune*, July 11, 1924.

"Canada's Most Wanted Criminals." *The Selkirk Enterprise,* February 15, 1961.

Dickie, Reid. "Manitoba Boogeyman Percy Moggey." readreidread.wordpress.com, September 26, 2011. https://readreidread.wordpress.com/?s=moggey

Fallding, Helen. "Town hoping crime pays: Eriksdale builds on 'Manitoba's Jesse James'." *Winnipeg Free Press*, July 29, 2000.

"Good News for a Lone Wolf." *Winnipeg Free Press*, August 18, 1960.

Guttormson, Elman. "Moggey appears in court, will face charge of escaping custody, perhaps others." *Winnipeg Free Press*, June 12, 1961.

Guttormson, Elman. "Moggey gets 2 more years." *Winnipeg Free Press*, June 16, 1961.

Guttormson, Elman. "Police capture Percy Moggey: Stony Mountain fugitive nabbed in hideout near Eriksdale." *Winnipeg Free Press*, June 10, 1961.

"Has Moggey jumped vast police dragnet? Cow may betray thirst-crazed prisoner." *Winnipeg Free Press*, July 27, 1960.

"Heat-struck Moggey gets 2 years extra." *The Winnipeg Tribune*, June 16, 1961.

"Helicopter joins hunt for escape prisoner: Convict scales 18-foot walls." *The Brandon Sun*, July 26, 1960.

"Life on Percy's private preserve: The neighbour was quiet," *The Winnipeg Tribune*, June 12, 1961.

"'Loner' Flees Pen, his 2nd escape from Stony Mountain." Winnipeg *Free Press*, July 25, 1960.

Manitoba Historical Society. "Historic Sites of Manitoba: Moggey Cabin." mhs.mb.ca. Last updated October 3, 2021. https://www.mhs.mb.ca/docs/sites/moggeycabin.shtml

Manitoba Historical Society. "Memorable Manitobans: Percy Charles Moggey." mhs.mb.ca, September 28, 2021. https://www.mhs.mb.ca/docs/people/moggey_p.shtml

"Master of jailbreaks, Moggey dies at 69." *Winnipeg Free Press*, August 17, 1974.

"Moggey faces charge of attempted murder: Man who shot two detectives also accused of about 20 different crimes." *Manitoba Free Press*, July 12, 1924.

"Moggey Foils Dragnet: Search shifts to Dauphin area." *Winnipeg Free Press*, July 28, 1960.

"Moggey's pals gain freedom." *The Winnipeg Tribune*, July 22, 1924.

"Mother spanks wayward son; police look on." *The Winnipeg Tribune*, July 8, 1924.

"'Myth' now 'Old Man': Moggey 4 years." *Winnipeg Free Press*, November 5, 1968.

"Percy Moggey: On the lam." *Winnipeg Tribune Magazine*, May 3, 1980.

"Police nab convicts in two hours: Penitentiary guard gets knife wound in futile break." *Winnipeg Free Press*, May 14, 1949.

"Retrace steps of Percy Moggey." *The Stonewall Argus*, June 10, 2002.

"Search for convict in Clear Lake area: Believed spotted north of Brandon." *The Brandon Sun*, July 27, 1960.

Seneca Root, Metismuseum.ca

Stozek, Ed. "Life of crime leads to Manitoba manhunt." *The Dauphin Herald*, November 12, 2019.

Unger, Erin. "Moggey's Mysterious Cabin by Eriksdale: A Convict's Tale." Mennotoba.com, July 22, 2020. https://www.mennotoba.com/moggeys-mysterious-cabin-by-eriksdale-a-convicts-tale/

Warms, John. *Over the Prison Wall: The Story of Percy Moggey*, Fairford, Manitoba: Roviera Publishing, 2001.

Weatherhead, Ted. "Moggey shot two detectives: Gun battle 36 years ago recalled." *Winnipeg Free Press*, September 6, 1960.

PUNKINHEAD: THE MANITOBA-MADE RIVAL TO RUDOLPH

Bernhardt, Darren. "From Snow White to Bugs Bunny: Gimli cottage was childhood home to artist who shaped cartoon history." cbc.ca, July 8, 2018. https://www.cbc.ca/news/canada/manitoba/gimli-home-cartoonist-charles-thorson-snow-white-bugs-bunny

Bernhardt, Darren. "When Winnipeg-created Punkinhead made Canadian retail history for Eaton's." cbc.ca December 27, 2020. https://www.cbc.ca/news/canada/manitoba/punkinhead-bear-cub-eatons-christmas-winnipeg-1.5840477

Bertolaccini, Bri. "Snow White and the Seven Dwarfs Honorary Academy Award." The Walt Disney Family Museum blog, February 23, 2023. https://www.waltdisney.org/blog/snow-white-and-seven-dwarfs-honorary-academy-awardr

Bowler, Gerry. *The World Encyclopedia of Christmas*, Toronto: McClelland & Stewart, 2000.

Britannica, T. Editors of Encyclopaedia. "Bugs Bunny." *Encyclopedia Britannica*, April 3, 2024. https://www.britannica.com/topic/Bugs-Bunny

Charlie Thorson fonds, University of Manitoba Archives and Special Collections

MacGregor, Roy. "The little bear from Eaton's catalogue of dreams." *The Globe and Mail,* December 24, 2007.

MacMillan, Robert. n.d. "Punkinhead" An Encyclopedia of Canadian Animation Cartooning and Illustration. https://canadianaci.ca/Encyclopedia/punkinhead/

"Punkinhead—Santa's Very Special Little Bear." n.d. Archives of Ontario. https://www.archives.gov.on.ca/en/explore/online/eatons/punkinhead.aspx

Vignal, Kristin (Thorson). "Charles (Charlie) Thorson." Icelandic National League of North America, June 4, 2013. https://inlofna.org/biographies/charles-thorson

HOW MANITOBANS AMPLIFIED ROCK 'N' ROLL

"American Jukebox History—Rock-Ola—History." n.d. https://www.jukeboxhistory.info/rock-ola/history.html.

Clayman, Andrew. "Rock-Ola MFG Corp., Est. 1927" Made-in-Chicago Museum, May 20, 2023. https://www.madeinchicagomuseum.com/single-post/rock-ola/

"David Cullen Rockola, Jukebox Inventor. Died on 25th January, 1993." eBrandon Discussion, January 25, 2012.https://ebrandon. ca/messagethread.aspx?message_id=583916&cat_id=57.

Einarson, John. "Sound by Garnet: Winnipeg's patron saint of rock 'n' roll drove city's sound." *The Winnipeg Free Press,* December 21, 2014.

Harding, Matt. "David Rockola Jukes His Way into Hall of Fame." *RePlay Magazine*, May 25, 2023.

Heise, Kenan. "Obituary: David C. Rockola, 96, jukebox manufacturer." ChicagoTribune.com, published January 27, 1993, last updated August 9, 2021. https://www.chicagotribune. com/1993/01/27/david-c-rockola-96-jukebox-manufacturer/

"Home of the Garnet Amplifier Company." n.d. http://www. garnetamps.com/

"Inventor amplified Winnipeg sound." Cbc.ca, January 8, 2007. https://www.cbc.ca/news/canada/manitoba/inventor-amplified-winnipeg-sound-1.636051

"King's cops swings in park Sunday." *The Winnipeg Tribune Showcase,* June 20, 1964.

Los Angeles Times. "David Rockola; Leading Maker of Jukeboxes." Latimes.com, March 8, 2019. https://www.latimes. com/archives/la-xpm-1993-01-28-mn-2225-story.html.

Manitoba Historical Society. "Memorable Manitobans: David Cullen Rockola." mhs.mb.ca, December 28, 2021. https://www.mhs.mb.ca/docs/people/rockola_dc.shtml

Manitoba Historical Society. "Memorable Manitobans: Thomas Garnett 'Gar' Gillies." mhs.mb.ca, May 26, 2016. https://www.mhs.mb.ca/docs/people/gillies_tg.shtml

"Manufacturer of Jukeboxes—David C. Rock-Ola Manufacturer of Jukeboxes." Rockola.co.uk. February 14, 2021. https://www.rockola.co.uk/.

Patriquin, Martin. n.d. "Thomas Garnet "Gar" Gillies: Musician, Sound Technician, Vacuum Tube Expert, Innovator, 1921-2006." *The Globe and Mail*

Preedy, Bob. "Obituary: David Rockola." *The Independent*, February 2, 1993. https://www.independent.co.uk/news/people/ obituary-david-rockola-1470478.html

"Rock-Ola—Jukebox Journey." n.d. https://jukeboxjourney.com/ history/rock-ola/

"Rock-Ola's Daring Dash to the Queen Mary." Rock-Ola. June 1, 2024. https://www.rock-ola.com/blogs/news/a-daring-dash-to-the-queen-mary

Thompson, Sam. "Portage Avenue mural honouring Winnipeg music legend taken down." Globalnews.ca, July 30, 2019. https://globalnews.ca/news/5697294/portage-avenue-mural-honouring-winnipeg-music-legend-disappears/

CHURCHILL'S MISSING GRAVITY

Aron, Jacob. "Gravity map reveals Earth's extremes." *New Scientist*, August 19, 2013. https://www.newscientist.com/ article/dn24068-gravity-map-reveals-earths-extremes

Borunda, Mario. "Why does gravity pull us down and not up?" theconversation.com, July 26, 2021. https://theconversation.com/why-does-gravity-pull-us-down-and-not-up

Bryner, Jeanna. "Weird Gravity in Canada Blamed on Hefty Glaciers." livescience.com, May 10, 2007. https://www.livescience.com/1507-weird-gravity-canada-blamed-hefty-glaciers.html

Donovan, John. "The Land That Gravity Forgot." Treehugger, June 5, 2017. https://www.treehugger.com/land-gravity-forgot-4863337

"GRACE Global Gravity Animation—GRACE Tellus." n.d. Jet Propulsion Laboratory, NASA/California Institute of Technology, July 17, 2009. https://grace.jpl.nasa.gov/resources/6/grace-global-gravity-animation

"Gravity Recovery and Climate Experiment (GRACE)," n.d. NASA. https://earthobservatory.nasa.gov/map#2/0.0/0.0

Helmholtz Association of German Research Centres. "*What Earth's gravity reveals about climate change.*" Phys.org, April 17, 2019. https://phys.org/news/2019-04-earth-gravity-reveals-climate.html

Jennings, Ken. "The Strange Reason You'll Always Weigh Less in Canada Than Anywhere Else." *Conde Nast Traveler*, April 14, 2014.

"Jerry X. Mitrovica: Theoretical Geophysicist." n.d. MacArthur Foundation. https://www.macfound.org/fellows/class-of-2019/jerry-x-mitrovica

Lodders, Katharina. *The planetary scientist's companion*, Oxford: Oxford University Press, 1998.

Manitoba Historical Society. "Historic Sites of Manitoba: Sloop Cove." mhs.mb.ca. Last updated October 16, 2019. https://www.mhs.mb.ca/docs/sites/sloopcove.shtml

Parks Canada. "History of Sloop Cove. Prince of Wales Fort National Historic Site." Ottawa: Government of Canada, April 18, 2024. https://parks.canada.ca/lhn-nhs/mb/prince/culture/decouvrir-discover3

Pratiksha. "Canada's Hudson Bay Has Less Gravity Than the Rest of the World." Curly Tales. November 20, 2019. https://curlytales.com/canada-hudson-bay-less-gravity

Scudder, Jillian. "How Do We Map the Earth's Gravity?" *Forbes Magazine*, March 30, 2017.

Silverman, Jacob. "How can parts of Canada be 'missing' gravity?" Howstuffworks.com, March 27, 2024. https://science.howstuffworks.com/environmental/earth/geophysics/missing-gravity.htm

Tapley, Benjamin. "Progress in Measuring the Earth's Gravity Field." *American Geophysical Union, Fall Meeting 2019*, December 2019.

Young, Kelly. "Satellites solve mystery of low gravity over Canada" *New Scientist*, May 10, 2007.

LEADING THE WAY: FIRSTS IN THE NORTHWEST

"A Winnipeg well which furnaces temperance beverages to the people." *Winnipeg Free Press*, December 23, 1893.

"About the Rev. Henry Budd." 2020. Henry Budd College for Ministry. November 10, 2020. https://henrybuddcollege.org/about-the-rev-henry-budd-2

Aird, Sir John. chairman, *Report of the Royal Commission on Radio Broadcasting*, Ottawa: Privy Council Office, 1929.

"Approval of first private network urged." *Winnipeg Free Press,* April 21, 1961.

Barkwell, Lawrence. "John Gunn," in *Metis Dictionary of Biography* Vol. D, Winnipeg: Louis Riel Institute, 2015.

Barkwell, Lawrence. "Métis Firsts in North America" excerpt from *Métis Legacy Vol. II: Michif Culture, Heritage, and Folkways.* Saskatoon: Gabriel Dumont Institute; Winnipeg: Pemmican Publications, 2006.

Barr, William. "Dr. John Rae's Telegraph Survey, St. Paul, Minnesota to Quesnel, British Columbia, 1864." *Manitoba History magazine,* No. 28 (Autumn/Winter 1999-2000). https://www.mhs.mb.ca/docs/mb_history/38/raetelegraphsurvey.shtml

Bateman, Tom. "Doctor brought the world to its knees." *Winnipeg Free Press.* February 23, 2016.

Begg, Alexander and Walter R. Nursey. *Ten Years in Winnipeg: A Narration of the Principal Events in the History of the City of Winnipeg from the Year A.D. 1870 to the Year A.D. 1879 Inclusive.* Winnipeg, 1879.

"Bell MTS: An Early History of Bell in Manitoba | BCE Inc." n.d. https://bce.ca/about-bce/history/bell-mts-an-early-history-of-bell-in-manitoba.

"The Birth and Death of The Canadian Radio Broadcasting Commission (1932-1936)" n.d. History of Canadian Broadcasting. Last updated July 2008. https://broadcasting-history.ca/radio/radio-networks/the-birth-and-death-of-the-canadian-radio-broadcasting-commission-1932-1936

"The Birthplace of the Anglican Church in Western Canada." St. John's Anglican Cathedral. July 22, 2020. https://stjohnscathedral.ca/about/our-past/history

Boon, T. C. B. "BUDD, HENRY," in *Dictionary of Canadian Biography*, vol. 10, University of Toronto/Université Laval, 2003–, accessed June 13, 2024. http://www.biographi.ca/en/bio/budd_henry_10E.html.

Boon, T.C.B. "Henry Budd, The First Native Indian Ordained in the Anglican Church on the North American Continent." *Manitoba Pageant.* Vol. 3, No. 1 (September 1957). https://www.mhs.mb.ca/docs/pageant/03/budd.shtml.

Bryce, George. *Early Days in Winnipeg.* Winnipeg: Manitoba Free Press, 1894.

Burchill, John. n.d. "At the End of the Rope." https://winnipegpolicemuseum.ca/wp-content/uploads/2021/03/at-the-end-of-the-rope.pdf.

Buvat, Dylan. "How a single flight from Winnipeg to The Pas forever changed the face of Canadian travel." n.d. Readers' Digest Canada. https://www.readersdigest.ca/travel/canada/first-commercial-flight/.

"Captain Frederick Joseph Stevenson: Canada's premier commercial pilot." plaque in Field of Honour section 150A, Brookside Cemetery, Winnipeg

Cassidy, Christian. "Manitoba's first patent: the pipe wrench." West End Dumplings (blog), July 25, 2011. https://westenddumplings.blogspot.com/2011/07/manitobas-first-patent-pipe-wrench.html.

Chang-Yen Phillips, Chris. "Canadians invented the garbage bag. Can we solve the mess they made?" cbc.ca, March 16, 2017. https://www.cbc.ca/2017/canadians-invented-the-garbage-bag-can-we-solve-the-mess-they-made-1.4024908

Cherney, Bruce. "Flight to The Pas—followed the Hudson Bay Railway to the community." *Winnipeg Regional Real Estate News.* June 30, 2016.

Cherney, Bruce. "Manitoba's first locomotive—the Countess of Dufferin arrived to bells, whistles and cheers." *Winnipeg Regional Real Estate News.* September 22, 2006.

Cherney, Bruce. "The 'Mother Club'—Granite Curling Club was formed in 1880 as a result of the 'battle between the rocks.'" *Winnipeg Regional Real Estate News.* December 9, 2011.

City of Winnipeg Heritage Resources

Coldwell, William and Scott Stephen. "Founding *The Nor'Wester.*" *Manitoba History Magazine.* No. 70 (Fall 2012). https://www.mhs.mb.ca/docs/mb_history/70/norwester.shtml

Collection of 1924 press clippings from Winnipeg's 50th anniversary celebrations. *Winnipeg in Focus*, City of Winnipeg Archives.

"The curling rink." *The Daily Free Press.* December 12, 1876.

"Delivery by bike: A relay race to Portage la Prairie Yesterday." *Manitoba Morning Free Press*, August 23, 1895.

Dickie, Reid. "The First Junior High." readreidread.wordpress.com, February 20, 2013. https://readreidread.wordpress.com/2013/02/20/the-first-junior-high-school

Dolyniuk, Maureen. *Muddy Waters: An interpretive guide to Winnipeg's Rivers.* Winnipeg: City of Winnipeg Parks and Recreation Department, 1982.

Dr. Elinor F. E. Black, University of Manitoba College of Medicine Archives

"Earl Grey School history." Winnipeg School Division. February 4, 2021. https://www.winnipegsd.ca/earlgrey/page/992/history

"Earl Grey School." n.d. Canadian Register of Historic Places. https://www.historicplaces.ca/en/rep-reg/place-lieu.aspx?id=6047

"Education makes gigantic leap in 38 years." *The Winnipeg Tribune*, June 30, 1909.

Even, Megan Lynn. "For over fifty years, steamboats plied the Red River." *MinnPost.* December 12, 2017. https://www.minnpost.com/mnopedia/2017/12/over-fifty-years-steamboats-plied-red-river/

"First Airmail/James Richardson/Bush Pilots." The Historical Marker Database. August 15, 2022. https://www.hmdb.org/m.asp?m=203816

"The First Christmas Tree in the Red River Settlement." *Winnipeg Free Press*. December 18, 1915.

Folkart, Burt A. "William Stephenson, 93; British Spymaster Dubbed 'Intrepid' Worked in U.S." *Los Angeles Times*, February 3, 1989.

Fraizer, Audrey. "Winnipeg—pioneer in 999." *The Journal of Emergency Dispatch*. February 7, 2021. https://www.iaedjournal.org/winnipeg-pioneer-in-999

"Froebe Helicopter—Royal Aviation Museum of Western Canada." Royal Aviation Museum of Western Canada. March 19, 2021. https://royalaviationmuseum.com/aircraft/froebe-helicopter/

Garland, Aileen. "The Nor'Wester and the Men Who Established It." *MHS Transactions,* Series 3 (1959-60). https://www.mhs.mb.ca/docs/transactions/3/norwester.shtml

"The Gateway to Rupert's Land" Hudson's Bay Company History Foundation.

Girard, Cheryl. "Shaarey Zedek has a long and proud history." *Winnipeg Free Press*. February 27, 2010.

Goldstein, Ken. "How Winnipeg Invented the Media." *Manitoba History Magazine*. No. 70 (Fall 2012). https://www.mhs.mb.ca/docs/mb_history/70/winnipegmedia.shtml

Government of Manitoba, *History of The Pas and Northern Manitoba*, 1969.

Government of Manitoba, Historic Resources Branch. *Manitoba Heritage Council Commemorative Plaques: Henry Budd*. https://www.gov.mb.ca/chc/hrb/plaques/plaq0152.html

Grebstad, David. "Winnipeg's First Execution." *Manitoba History Magazine*. No. 86 (Winter 2018). https://www.mhs.mb.ca/docs/mb_history/86/winnipegexecution.shtml

Gwiazda, Emily. "Marie-Anne Lagimodière." *The Canadian Encyclopedia*. Historica Canada. Article published January 20, 2008; Last Edited January 26, 2023. https://www.thecanadianencyclopedia.ca/en/article/marie-anne-lagemodiere

Hartman, James B. "The Golden Age of the Organ in Manitoba: 1875-1919." *Manitoba History Magazine.* No. 29 (Spring 1995). https://www.mhs.mb.ca/docs/mb_history/29/goldenageoforgans.shtml

Healy, William James. *Winnipeg's Early Days*. Winnipeg: Stovel Company Ltd., 1927.

Heeney, William Bertal. *John West and his Red River mission.* Toronto: The Musson Book Company Ltd., 1920. http://anglicanhistory.org/canada/heeney_west.html

Heritage Winnipeg. "100 Years Young: The Marlborough Hotel." Heritage Winnipeg Blog, October 29, 2014.

Heritage Winnipeg. "Our First and Last Streetcars." Heritage Winnipeg Blog.

History of Canadian Broadcasting: https://broadcasting-history.ca/

"History of Harlequin Enterprises Limited." n.d. Funding Universe. http://www.fundinguniverse.com/company-histories/harlequin-enterprises-limited-history/.

"History, Winnipeg Music Festival." n.d. Winnipeg Music Festival. https://www.winnipegmusicfestival.org/history

"Homewood, Manitoba, honors flight of first Canadian helicopter." *Vertical Magazine*. August 29, 2018. https://verticalmag.com/news/homewood-manitoba-honors-flight-of-first-helicopter-in-canada

"Inside the Winnipeg Police Service: celebrating the origins of 911." City of Winnipeg

"Institute discusses ways to foster inter-racial goodwill." *Winnipeg Tribune*. November 14, 1949.

The Intrepid Society: intrepid-society.org

Janke, Donna. "Policing and Social History at Winnipeg Police Museum." Destinations, Detours and Dreams. January 27, 2019. https://www.destinationsdetoursdreams.com/2019/01/policing-and-social-history-at-winnipeg-police-museum/

Knafla, Louis A. and Jonathan Swainger, eds. *Laws and Societies in the Canadian Prairie West, 1670-1940*, Vancouver: UBC Press, 2005.

Laychuk, Riley. *Manitoba-born pioneer who 'set the stage' for knee replacements passes away*, CBC News, Feb. 23, 2016.

Loose Rivets: The story of Fred Wilmot and Burrard Dry Dock, Museum and Archives of North Vancouver/monova.ca

Lowrie-Chin, Jean. *Fred and Cynthia Wilmot—life on their own terms*, Jamaica Observer, March 3, 2008.

Lowrie-Chin, Jean. *Unforgettable Fred Wilmot*, Jamaica Observer, Sept. 5, 2016.

Lucas, Fred C. *Historical Diary of Winnipeg*, published by Cartwright and Lucas, Winnipeg, 1923.

Macdonald, Bill. *The True Intrepid: Sir William Stephenson and the unknown agents*, Timberholme Books Ltd., 1998.

Manitoba Archives. n.d. "Extracts from registers of baptisms, marriages and burials in Rupert's Land sent to the Governor and Committee (1820-1851)." https://www.gov.mb.ca/chc/archives/hbca/name_indexes/rrs_baptisms_marriages_burials.html

Manitoba Archives. "Manitoba Society of Artists"

"Manitoba Club history." n.d. Manitoba Club. https://manitobaclub.mb.ca/history

Manitoba Historical Society. "Central Schools / Victoria-Albert School." Mhs.mb.ca, Last updated November 3, 2023. https://www.mhs.mb.ca/docs/sites/victoriaalbertschool.shtml

Manitoba Historical Society. "Earl Grey School." Mhs.mb.ca, Last updated February 11, 2024. https://www.mhs.mb.ca/docs/sites/earlgreyschool.shtml

Manitoba Historical Society. "First Airmail Flight in Manitoba (Lac du Bonnet)." Mhs.mb.ca, Last updated January 31, 2021. https://www.mhs.mb.ca/docs/sites/firstairmail.shtml

Manitoba Historical Society. "First School in Winnipeg (39 Maple Street)." Mhs.mb.ca, Last updated April 21, 2021. https://www.mhs.mb.ca/docs/sites/winnipegfirstschool.shtml

Manitoba Historical Society. "The Nor'Wester / Manitoba Hotel / Industrial Bureau Exposition Building / Federal Building (269 Main Street)." Mhs.mb.ca, Last updated June 2, 2024. https://www.mhs.mb.ca/docs/sites/norwester.shtml

Manitoba Historical Society. "Trans-Canada Highway Monument (Eastern Manitoba)." Mhs.mb.ca, Last updated July 2, 2023. https://www.mhs.mb.ca/docs/sites/transcanadahighway.shtml

Manitoba Historical Society. "Alice Edith Ostrander." mhs.mb.ca, January 10, 2022. https://www.mhs.mb.ca/docs/people/ostrander_a.shtml

Manitoba Historical Society. "Elinor Frances Elizabeth Black." mhs.mb.ca, March 29, 2022. https://www.mhs.mb.ca/docs/people/black_efe.shtml

Manitoba Historical Society. "Elizabeth Dundas Long." mhs.mb.ca, July 25, 2023. https://www.mhs.mb.ca/docs/people/long_ed.shtml

Manitoba Historical Society. "Frederick Joseph Stevenson." mhs.mb.ca, March 9, 2024. https://www.mhs.mb.ca/docs/people/stevenson_fj.shtml

Manitoba Historical Society. "Harry Wasylyk." mhs.mb.ca, November 8, 2021. https://www.mhs.mb.ca/docs/people/wasylyk_h.shtml

Manitoba Historical Society. "Horace McDougall." mhs.mb.ca, April 8, 2021. https://www.mhs.mb.ca/docs/people/mcdougall_h.shtml

Manitoba Historical Society. "Irvine "Irv" Robbins." mhs.mb.ca, May 31, 2024. https://www.mhs.mb.ca/docs/people/robbins_i.shtml

Manitoba Historical Society. "John S. Ingram." mhs.mb.ca, July 25, 2018. https://www.mhs.mb.ca/docs/people/ingram_js.shtml

Manitoba Historical Society. "Josefina Asgerdur Kristjanson." mhs.mb.ca, July 25, 2018. https://www.mhs.mb.ca/docs/people/ingram_js.shtml

Manitoba Historical Society. "Mary Annie Wawrykow." mhs.mb.ca, April 23, 2024. https://www.mhs.mb.ca/docs/people/wawrykow_ma.shtml

Manitoba Historical Society. "Mary Margaret 'Margery' Brooker." mhs.mb.ca, August 9, 2022. https://www.mhs.mb.ca/docs/people/brooker_mm.shtml

Manitoba Historical Society. "Olive Lillian Irvine." mhs.mb.ca, December 10, 2021. https://www.mhs.mb.ca/docs/people/irvine_ol.shtml

Manitoba Historical Society. "Richard Henry Gardyne Bonnycastle." mhs.mb.ca, April 1, 2023. https://www.mhs.mb.ca/docs/people/bonnycastle_rhg.shtml

Manitoba Historical Society. "Thomas Ryan." mhs.mb.ca, April 21, 219. https://www.mhs.mb.ca/docs/people/ryan_t.shtml

Manitoba Historical Society. "William Hespeler." mhs.mb.ca, November 4, 2020. https://www.mhs.mb.ca/docs/people/hespeler_w.shtml

"Manitoba Organization: Winnipeg Canoe Club." Manitoba Historical Society Archives. August 21, 2023. https://www.mhs.mb.ca/docs/organization/winnipegcanoeclub.shtml

McFadden, Molly. "Steamboating on the Red." *MHS Transactions*, Series 3 (1950-51). https://www.mhs.mb.ca/docs/transactions/3/steamboating.shtml

McLeod, James Dudley. N.d. "Personal Memoirs: The Story of Earl Grey School 1952." Mhs.mb.ca. Last updated May 16, 2015. https://www.mhs.mb.ca/docs/memoirs/earlgreyschool/index.shtml

Melady, John. *Breakthrough! Canada's Greatest Inventions and Innovations*. Toronto: Dundurn Press, 2013.

Morrison, Fred. "First Lady of the Rails." *Manitoba Pageant,* Vol. 4, No. 1 (September 1958). https://www.mhs.mb.ca/docs/pageant/04/ladyoftherails.shtml

Mott, Morris and John Allardyce. *Curling Capital: Winnipeg and the Roarin' Game, 1876 to 1988*, Winnipeg: University of Manitoba Press, 1989.

Muir, Gilbert A. "A History of the Telephone in Manitoba." *MHS Transactions,* Series 3 (1964-1965). https://mhs.mb.ca/docs/transactions/3/telephone.shtml

Museum, Miami Railway Station. n.d. "Miami Railway Station Museum." Miami Railway Station Museum. https://miamirailwaystationmuseum.com/telephones.

Nash, Knowlton. *The Microphone Wars*. Toronto: McClelland and Stewart, 1994.

Nelson, Valerie J. "Irvine Robbins, 90; co-founder of the Baskin- Robbins ice cream empire." *Los Angeles Times*, September 16, 2014.

Nichols, Mark Edgar. *The Story of The Canadian Press*, Whitby: Ryerson Press, 1948.

"On Gunston's Knee." *North Roots Magazine*, October/November 2009.

Orr, John L. "From sea to sea, by air: The first trans-Canada flight." *Skies Magazine,* October 19, 2020.

"Our first circus: Its unfortunate career and inglorious end." *Manitoba Free Press,* July 6, 1878.

"Our History—the Royal Canadian Legion." n.d. https://legion.ca/who-we-are/what-we-do/our-history

"Our History." n.d. Winnipeg Airports Authority. https://www.ywg.ca/en/corporate/about-us/our-history

Parks Canada. "Commemorating the First Railway in Western Canada." *Manitoba History Magazine,* No. 58 June 2008. https://www.mhs.mb.ca/docs/mb_history/58/firstrailway.shtml

Parks Canada. "The Construction of the Trans-Canada Highway." Canada.Ca. February 15, 2016. https://www.canada.ca/en/parks-canada/news/2016/02/the-construction-of-the-trans-canada-highway.html.

Parks Canada. "History of Sloop Cove. Prince of Wales Fort National Historic Site." Ottawa: Government of Canada, April 18, 2024. https://parks.canada.ca/lhn-nhs/mb/prince/culture/decouvrir-discover3

Parks Canada Directory of Federal Heritage Designations. n.d. "Founding of The Royal Canadian Legion National Historic Event." Government of Canada. https://www.pc.gc.ca/apps/dfhd/page_nhs_eng.aspx?id=12538

Paterson, Edith. *Tales of Early Manitoba from the Winnipeg Free Press*. Winnipeg: Winnipeg Free Press, 1970.

Petite, Bob. "Vertical Rewind: The flying Froebes." *Vertical Magazine*, August 2, 2018.

Phillipson, Donald J.C. "Sir William Stephenson." *The Canadian Encyclopedia*. Historica Canada. Article published January 23, 2008; Last Edited March 04, 2015. https://www.thecanadianencyclopedia.ca/en/article/sir-william-stephenson

Rea, J.E. "Anson Northup." *The Canadian Encyclopedia*. Historica Canada. Article published February 06, 2006; Last Edited December 16, 2013. https://www.thecanadianencyclopedia.ca/en/article/anson-northup

Render, Shirley. "Stevenson, Frederick Joseph," in *Dictionary of Canadian Biography*, vol. 15, University of Toronto/Université Laval, 2003–, accessed June 13, 2024, http://www.biographi.ca/en/bio/stevenson_frederick_joseph_15E.html.

Reynolds, George F. "The Man Who Created the Corner of Portage and Main." *MHS Transactions*, Series 3, No. 26 (1969-70 season). https://www.mhs.mb.ca/docs/transactions/3/portageandmain.shtml

"Robert Leckie." Canada's Aviation Hall of Fame. May 12, 2021. https://cahf.ca/robert-leckie.

"Ryan's Boot & Shoe Store." n.d. Seven Oaks & Ross House Museum. http://www.sevenoakshouse.ca/ryans-boot--shoe-store.html

Sallis, Josephine. "Reading Behind the Lines: Archiving the Canadian News Media Record." A thesis submitted to the Faculty of Graduate Studies of the University of Manitoba, 2013

Segal, David. "A Reader's Digest That Grandma Never Dreamed Of." nytimes.com, December 20, 2009.

Sharp, Tim. "The world's first commercial airline." Space.com, February 28, 2022. https://www.space.com/16657-worlds-first-commercial-airline-the-greatest-moments-in-flight.html

"Sir William Stephenson: The man called Intrepid." n.d. Winnipeg Regional Real Estate Board. https://www.winnipegregionalrealestateboard.ca/community/citizens-hall-of-fame/inductee/43/Sir-William-Stephenson

Smythe, Terry. "William Samuel Stephenson." n.d. *Encyclopedia of the Great Plains*. University of Nebraska-Lincoln. http://plainshumanities.unl.edu/encyclopedia/doc/egp.war.045

"Steamboats, 1859-1871 | Fargo History." n.d. North Dakota State University Archives. https://library.ndsu.edu/fargo-history/index33f1.html?q=content/steamboats-1859-1871.

"Stephenson. William Stephenson." *UM Today, the magazine.* Fall 2017. https://news.umanitoba.ca/stephenson-william-stephenson/

Stevenson, William. *A Man Called Intrepid*, Connecticut: The Lyons Press, 1976.

Stouffer, Garth. "Man of mystery; Norman Breakey, paint roller inventor." *Brandon Sun*, April 19, 1975.

Stubbs, Roy St. George. *Four Recorders of Rupert's Land: A brief Survey of the Hudson's Bay Company Courts of Rupert's Land*, Winnipeg: Peguis Publishers, 1967.

Templeman, Jack. "The Early 1900s." Winnipeg Police Museum. March 2021. https://winnipegpolicemuseum.ca/wp-content/uploads/2021/03/The-Roaring-20s.pdf

Templeman, Jack. "Winnipeg's first official lawmen." Winnipeg Police Museum. March 2021. https://winnipegpolicemuseum.ca/wp-content/uploads/2021/03/New-Frontier.pdf

"The Story of Manitoba: A Brief History of Manitoba from 1612 to 1890." *The Winnipeg Tribune*, July 14, 1970.

"There's nothing trashy about the history of trash bags." AAA Polymer, Inc. December 17, 2019. https://www.aaapolymer.com/history-of-trash-bags/

Town of Niverville: www.whereyoubelong.ca/living-here/about

"Victoria-Albert School History." Winnipeg School Division. September 19, 2022. https://www.winnipegsd.ca/victoria-albert/page/3854/history

Wade, Jill. "BEGG, ALEXANDER (1825-1905)," in *Dictionary of Canadian Biography*, vol. 13, University of Toronto/Université Laval, 2003–, accessed June 13, 2024, http://www.biographi.ca/en/bio/begg_alexander_1825_1905_13E.html.

Welch, Deborah , and Michael Payne. "Niverville." *The Canadian Encyclopedia*. Historica Canada. Article published September 11, 2012; Last Edited March 04, 2015. https://www.thecanadianencyclopedia.ca/en/article/niverville

"William Stephenson." n.d. Spartacus Educational. https://spartacus-educational.com/2WWstephensonW.html

Winnipeg Art Gallery: www.wag.ca

"Winnipeg-Kenora Highway opened following boundary ceremonies" *The Winnipeg Evening Tribune,* July 2, 1935.

Wright, Glenn T. "Royal Canadian Legion." *The Canadian Encyclopedia*. Historica Canada. Article published March 16, 2009; Last Edited June 18, 2022. https://www.thecanadianencyclopedia.ca/en/article/royal-canadian-legion

THE LAST OF THE BUFFALO   NEAR WINNIPEG, MAN.

An undated postcard showing a herd of bison near Winnipeg
says they are "the last of the buffalo." COURTESY DARREN BERNHARDT